TOTAL VICTORY

Sunzi's Art of Business

Written & illustrated by **Wang Xuanming**

Translated by **Foo Choo Yen**

ASIAPAC • SINGAPORE

Publisher
ASIAPAC BOOKS PTE LTD
996 Bendemeer Road #06-09 Singapore 339944
Tel: (65) 6392 8455 Fax: (65) 6392 6455
Email asiapacbooks@pacific.net.sg

Visit us at our Internet home page
www.asiapacbooks.com

First published November 2005

© 2005 ASIAPAC BOOKS, SINGAPORE
ISBN 981-229-404-X

All rights reserved. No part of this publication may be reproduced, stored in a retrieval system, or transmitted, in any form or by any means, electronic, mechanical, photocopying, recording, or otherwise, without the prior written permission of the publisher. Under no circumstances shall it be rented, resold or redistributed. If this copy is defective, kindly exchange it at the above address.

Cover design: Pyxis Communications & Consultancy Pte Ltd
Page Layout: Wong Seow Wee
Body text: 9 pt Helvetica
Printer: Loi Printing Pte Ltd

Publisher's Note

Sunzi's Art of War is an enduring military classic that has greatly influenced the world. The principles of strategising and the secret to winning battles contained in the classic can be applied to state administration, business management, public relations, diplomacy as well as everyday life.

This new book *Total Victory - Sunzi's Art of Business* depicts 100 case studies in businesses and demonstrates how entrepreneurs and businessmen have employed the principles of *Sunzi's Art of War* to thrive and stay ahead in the fast-changing and competitive business environment. There are 100 case studies, with stories of well-known entrepreneurs like Lee Iacocca, Andrew Carnegie, John D. Rockefeller, Li Ka-Shing, Lee Kong Chian, Tan Kah Kee, etc. Famous Asian and western corporations like Nissan, Honda, Nokia, Hewlett-Packard Computers, Philips Electronics, Casio, etc. are featured as well, illustrating the credibility of Sunzi's strategic art of business.

"Treat the captured good soldiers well." Sunzi believed that to manage an army begins with caring for the army. To lead an army is to lead through the heart and not through the use of force. In business, human resources are the most important element in an organization. Treat the employees well and they will devote themselves to the company and perform their best.

To succeed in business, an entrepreneur must "know oneself", which means understanding his company and the situation surrounding him, and "know others", which refers to knowing market changes, consumers' psychology and his competitors. Although *Sunzi's Art of War* is very much military in nature, Sunzi did not expect good success in battles all the time. On the contrary, his strategies are concerned with minimising losses as well.

We thank the author-illustrator, Wang Xuanming, for granting us the honour of publishing this book. We also thank Foo Choo Yen for his translation and the production team for their hard work in putting this volume together.

About the Illustrator

Wang Xuanming 王宣铭, a contemporary cartoonist in China, was born in Beijing in 1950. He was trained formally in commercial art and industrial art. Since 1972, he has been engaged in various aspects of artistic work. He frequently explores various ways of expressing his artistic talents. Besides a lot of cartoons, picture books and illustrations, he makes oil paintings and posters. His works have on many occasions won awards in several art competitions and have been included in various art albums.

Wang's works have been serialised in all the major newspapers and publications in Beijing since 1980. His cartoons entitled *Different Gravitational Force* are praised by famous Chinese artists. In 1987, he participated in the creation of the animated cartoon *Brother Elephant*, which won the hearts of many children when it first appeared on television.

In his Strategy and Leadership Series, he uses a simple and humorous art form to introduce ancient Chinese military classics to modern readers. The books were very well received when they were first published in China; the Beijing Radio Station reviewed and highly recommended them to the public.

Preface

"The most brilliant tactic is not to win a hundred hard-fought battles but to subdue the enemy without going to war." — This philosophy was clearly expounded by the ancient Chinese military strategist, Sunzi, in his masterpiece *Sunzi's Art of War* more than 2500 years ago. In his writings, Sunzi objected to direct engagement as a means to achieve strategic objectives. Instead, he accentuated the use of stratagems and subtly making use of power and resourcefulness for strategic realization of "war without conflict". This exciting strategic thinking has spread far and wide through the ages. *Sunzi's Art of War* received worldwide attention and is a subject of research and study. Currently, *Sunzi's Art of War* has transcended military application and is being used in areas as varied as politics, diplomacy, economics and business management. It has also found its application in competitive sports. The teachings found in *Sunzi's Art of War* have become a major subject of study in many military academies and business schools. According to statistics, the subject matter that commands the most reading interest among entrepreneurs is *Sunzi's Art of War*.

Competition is here to stay for everyone. Competition is a fact of life and a driver for social development. For a country, an enterprise and even for an individual, the road to survival, progress and victory depends on whether one is able to out-manoeuvre competitors and prove his worth and strengthen his capability in the competition. Those who dare not face up and shy away from competition will be drowned in oblivion in the tide of times.

The hard truth is, for one to become the most powerful and eventual winner in a competition, he needs to feel the rhythms of competition, master the intricacies in the arts in competition and be equipped with the competitive capability. *Sunzi's Art of War* can be a beacon of light in enlightening these aspects.

While Sunzi incisively explained the rhythm of competition, he proposed a series of unique and valuable stratagems for victory. For example, Sunzi wrote "Precise knowledge of self and precise knowledge of enemy leads to victory." He clearly suggested that to win in competition, one needs to be aware of our situation and the opponent's. This has been a basis in competition and has gained more importance in this age of information.

Undoubtedly, the current age is an era of competition for an individual, an enterprise and also for a country. The environment we are living in is undergoing a massive transformation and major changes are taking place. This is an era of quickened pace and speedy development where science, technology and beliefs are constantly evolving. It is indeed an era of contradictions and risks; a true representation of "survival of the fittest". The fittest will achieve miraculous success but the weaker ones will sink deep into the trappings of defeat and be purged out in the ruthless game of survival.

This competition of age is dynamic and is always changing. The contradictions in things once taken for granted are getting more obvious and there are more hidden pitfalls of troubles. The elements of uncertainty and risks are especially prominent. We can see many results of competition that ended not with an "ultimate win" but a dismal outcome of "mutual defeat" and "losses outstripping gains". In many instances, we could not get the intended returns but paid an even heavier price for competition. The increased competition, new-found opportunities and emerging challenges, coupled with the quest for fabled victories and glorious successes have drastically altered the rules of the games. People who intend to compete must be hungry to learn the rhythm of competition and possess the capabilities for victory.

Sunzi's Art of War helps direct us out of the competition maze by revealing the secret of success through a series of thought-provoking conceptions that ply on "defeating the muscular with brain", "defeating the steely with gentleness" and "victory without a fight". The application in the current era has never been so prominent before.

Sunzi's Art of War elevated competition to a high level of rational reasoning and position competition into the scope of a wider strategic boundary. The philosophy emphasized the righteousness in the use of force and put morality as the criterion for competition. In all attempts, we must minimize the damages from conflicts of power and achieve successes with minimum cost.

Sunzi's Art of War has greatly enriched and opened up our thoughts and beliefs and is a valuable wealth in spirit and soul. In *Sunzi's Art of War*, ruthless competition is subjected to the rules of rational thinking and mindless conflict is confined within an ordered framework. People who have mastered these concepts can correctly set the competitive objectives, identify the opponents and strategize the competitive tactics. On top of these, limiting the scope and length of competition causes the least damage upon oneself and minimize the negative impact on society.

The competition endorsed in *Sunzi's Art of War* is one that adheres to humanity and suits the characteristics and requirements of the present age. It is widely promoted by strategists of this era. It leads every reader to believe: One is able to stay undefeated in the heat of competition!

This is what this book has set out to achieve too.

Introduction

Sunzi's Art of War contains a mere 5000 Chinese characters. The content, however, is all-encompassing and deep in essence. The book touches on a wide range of topics such as war, politics, economics and diplomacy. It is indeed a treasure for writings of stratagems. It has been more than 2500 years since Sunzi wrote the military stratagems but the book has gained ever wider and deeper interest.

Japanese entrepreneurs were the first to put into practice the stratagems and philosophies contained in *Sunzi's Art of War* to enterprise management and business competition. Historical records documented that the Japanese scholar, Kibino Makibi, first visited China in AD716 to study economics and history. After nineteen years of study in China, he brought back to Japan ancient books and manuscripts, including *Sunzi's Art of War,* which became the secret manuals for the Japanese dynasty. The Japanese scholars and warriors were enthralled with reading and studying Chinese military writings, especially *Sunzi's Art of War*. In the Japanese publication *The Values of Sunzi's Art of War in Modern Society*, it was suggested that it is the "book that transcends all times" among the Chinese ancient military books. It further referred to Sunzi as the "Sage of Oriental Military Strategy". Many Japanese industrial founders and learned scholars spent many important years researching and actively applying stratagems from *Sunzi's Art of War* into Japanese enterprise management and business competition. The Japanese companies accumulated profound experience and created an economic wonder of the world.

The Japanese entrepreneur, Oohashi Takeo, took over a small factory in Koishikikawa and successfully transformed it into the world renowned Toyo Precision Parts Manufacturing Company Limited. Among his books on management successes such as *Managing with Military Strategies*, Oohashi credited his accomplishments to the use of stratagems described in *Sunzi's Art of War* like "accurate forecast", "anticipate the enemy", "empower the commanders", "winning the hearts", "striking out at opportunities", "unanticipated moves", "united in hearts we triumph" and "win without fighting". The management at Sony Corporation affirmed that the great achievements Sony realized within a short forty-five year period was in its successful implementation of the principles in the "Arts of Qi and Zheng" (奇正之术). Sony continually introduces new products that are good in quality and value for money.

The famous Japanese entrepreneur Matsushita Konosuke mentioned that he was able to transform his small workshop in 1918 to a corporate giant that has more than 130 plants and factories across the five continents largely due to the teachings in

Sunzi's Art of War. He further said: "Chinese ancient philosopher, Sunzi, is the supreme immortal. Our company's employees must pay tribute to him and seriously learn and apply his teachings. Then only can we be successful and prosperous."

There are many other similar instances and anecdotes. Japanese academic, Murayama, rightfully pointed out: There are two pillars of survival and progress for Japanese enterprises. One is the American modern management system. The other is the use of the tactics and strategies found in *Sunzi's Art of War*. Take a quick look at the many examples within the Japanese industry and we can quickly conclude that the stratagems and philosophies in *Sunzi's Art of War* are fully applicable to modern enterprise management and business competition. The successes achieved are remarkable.

The last few years witnessed great changes in the business environment. We may use the following two descriptions to summarize the business environment in the 21st century: *chaos* and *confusion*. The strong tide of change seemingly destroyed everything and business opportunities came and vanished in no time. Incomplete information further confounded the blurred and hazy situation. It is definitely stressful for every manager working under these conditions.

With the current state of affairs, we need to revisit past theories, look for new interpretation on what competition is and re-establish the operating system and model. In short, the dynamic competition warrants a new rational guidance.

Sunzi's Art of War is not about providing a set of mechanical and rigid creeds to be followed by the entrepreneurs but is an instinctive guidance. This guidance helps entrepreneurs proactively and nimbly react to the complex situations. It is exactly this high level of abstractness, compactness and summarized characteristics that give *Sunzi's Art of War* an advantage in giving a holistic view on applicable strategies in the current age.

From a philosophical aspect, *Sunzi's Art of War* fully explains the common laws that govern conflict of power and competition. It suggests a scientific approach to apply one's power, working within the whole system, to achieve victorious objectives. *Sunzi's Art of War* provides a realistic methodological guidance for entrepreneurs through its cohesive, abstract and instinctive approach. This approach gives profound enlightenment and wider assimilation of ideas. The language used in *Sunzi's Art of War* is very concise and vividly describes the overall competitive strategies. It further unveils the true elements and logical framework of competitive strategies. It can hence be said that *Sunzi's Art of War* is no longer simply a masterpiece on warfare but a truly enlightening ideological work applicable to many aspects, especially in business competition.

This masterpiece does not only explain the basic principles on how to compete, it further elaborates how these basic principles function under correct moral values. The strong belief in harmony and peace elucidated in *Sunzi's Art of War* has received wide acceptance by many people. Applying the stratagems in today's economic competition, is in itself a modern realization of peaceful use of this military book. We must apply *Sunzi's Art of War* in a peaceful manner and confine competition within a framework of logic and rationale.

Competitive strategy is a profound knowledge; the true essence of war strategy is not easily understood by simple rationale. It is insufficient to rely solely on the explanation and examples in this book to master the principles in *Sunzi's Art of War* at a strategic level. Some of the abstruse strategy cannot be lucidly explained in common terms. This would require the readers to exercise their initiative to master and apply some special cognitive methods often used by other strategists. One of the cognitive methods is what is described by the Chinese strategists as "realization"(悟). This means to use one's sub-consciousness to master some deep principles. This sub-consciousness builds on actual practices and experiences, for one to apply his discerning ability to "realize" the deep meanings within the words. To study *Sunzi's Art of War* is not a one-time affair. One needs to learn progressively with improvement in the level of understanding after numerous experiences and reflections. This will continuously bring us closer to the significance contained within *Sunzi's Art of War*.

Contents

Chapter 1	**The Entrepreneur**	1
Section 1	What is an entrepreneur?	
Section 2	Moral upbringing of an entrepreneur	
Section 3	Dangerous traits of an entrepreneur	
Chapter 2	**Managing the Employees**	21
Section 1	Empowerment	
Section 2	The way of employment, administration and operation	
Section 3	Harmonious communication	
Chapter 3	**Strategy for Company Talents**	41
Section 1	Knowing and deploying talents	
Section 2	Improving the quality of employees and training for talents	
Section 3	Sincerity towards employees	
Chapter 4	**The Art of Formulating Strategy**	59
Section 1	A winning mentality	
Section 2	Achieving victory without a fight	
Section 3	Thorough analysis before setting targets	
Section 4	Technology advancement is an edge for business competition	
Chapter 5	**Competitive Strategy for Company**	86
Section 1	Operating cost advantage	
Section 2	Winning by surprise	
Section 3	Strategy of partial competition	

Chapter 6 **Competitive Strategy in Business** 102
Section 1 *Enterprising attack and active defence*
Section 2 *Insist on quality and dare to innovate*
Section 3 *Strategy in price psychology*
Section 4 *Attack on weaknesses. Explore new markets*

Chapter 7 **Market and Information Analysis** 127
Section 1 *Adjust product and services to changes*
Section 2 *Analyze the environment and know your competitors*
Section 3 *Analyze the overall market scientifically and accurately*

Chapter 8 **Business Competition** 149
Section 1 *Seize the business opportunity*
Section 2 *Looking for the best returns*
Section 3 *Dealing with uncertainties*

Chapter 9 **Art of Establishing Business Relationship
and Negotiation** 166
Section 1 *Negotiation is an important technique in business*
Section 2 *The techniques of negotiation*

Chapter 10 **Building a Corporate Culture** 181
Section 1 *Establish common ideals and team spirit*
Section 2 *Be a responsible corporate citizen*

Chapter 1
The Entrepreneur

Section 1 Who is an entrepreneur?

Section 2 Moral upbringing of an entrepreneur

Section 3 Dangerous traits of an entrepreneur

The Entrepreneur
Section 1　Who is an entrepreneur?

> 夫将者，国之辅也。辅周则国必强，辅隙则国必弱。
> A general is the safeguard of the nation.
> When this support is in place, the nation will certainly be strong.
> When this support is not in place, the nation will certainly be weak.
> 　　　　　　　　　— *Chapter: Attack by Stratagem*　《谋攻篇》
>
> 故知兵之将，民之司命。国家安危之主也。
> A general who understands warfare is the guardian of civilians' lives, and the head of the nation's security.
> 　　　　　　　　　— *Chapter: Waging War*　《作战篇》
>
> 料敌制胜，计险阨远近，上将之道也。
> Anticipate the enemy's moves, create conditions leading to victory, calculating the dangers and distances. These are the Ways of the superior general.
> 　　　　　　　　　— *Chapter: The Terrain*　《地形篇》

A general is a key safeguard to a country's peace and prosperity. A responsible and courageous general will make a country strong and prosperous. An irresponsible general who harbours ulterior motives will lead to the downfall of a country.

Hence, a general skilled in utilizing his armies is the guardian for its people and pillar to the security of a nation. A good general is able to anticipate his enemies, plan his moves by knowing the terrain and by calculating the journey his soldiers need to make. These are the responsibilities of a general.

An entrepreneur is the master of an enterprise. In a sense, he is the company's general. The entrepreneur needs to have a broad view of the entire situation, while controlling the key issues and making the right decisions.

An entrepreneur without a lucid mind cannot make intelligent decisions and will steer his ship into storms and turmoil. The ship will travel in a sea of submerged reefs and will be in danger of wreckage. He cannot sustain good business and lead his company forward.

Case Study 1: A Hands-On Entrepreneur Revived An Ailing Enterprise

After leaving Ford in 1978, Lee Iacocca was aggressively courted by Chrysler Corporation. The car maker was on the verge of collapse. Iacocca joined Chrysler and began rebuilding the company.

The amount of debt at that time was a whopping USD 4.8 billion.

In 1979, the loss was USD 1.1 billion.

In 1978, the loss was USD 204 million.

After arriving in Chrysler, Iacocca announced:

Before the company turns into profitability, I am forgoing my paycheck of USD 360,000. I will draw USD 1 as annual salary.

Iacocca discovered that the company was grossly mis-managed. Many positions were redundant.

Good gracious! There are 35 vice presidents in this company!

In the following three years he retrenched 33 vice presidents.

To obtain funds for sustaining the operations, Iacocca approached the United States Congress for a loan guarantee.

We can give you a loan guarantee of USD 1.5 billion!

I am deeply appreciative!

To cut cost and expenses, Iacocca went on an extensive retrenchment and salary cutting campaign.

"I give you my promise. Once the company turns around, I will re-adjust your paycheck!"

Employment expenses: Cut from USD 2.1 billion to USD 1.5 billion. A total of 1,700 senior executives had a salary reduction of 10%. Ordinary employees had a salary reduction of 2% — 5%. The annual inventory was reduced from USD 2.1 billion to USD 1.2 billion.

"The production of the convertibles has stopped for six years. There is a revival of interest for this design of cars. Let's produce 3,000 convertibles for the market as a trial."

Iacocca had the first mover's advantage by anticipating the change in consumer's preference. Chrysler first rolled out the "DODGE 400" convertible model in 1982. Soon, the sales surpassed the 23,000 figure. Thereafter, other automakers like General Motors and Ford went into the production of convertibles too. This was the first time Chrysler took the lead.

"We constantly seek innovation in design, colours and features. These changes are welcomed by the consumers."

In designing a new car, there were two important aspects: design improvement and technology improvement. Design improvement was cheaper to make and gave quick results with short product life cycles. Iacocca made design improvement as Chrysler's strategic focus.

The keys for the success of an enterprise are creativity, inventiveness and transformation. The entrepreneur needs to exercise a unique sales and marketing strategy for the product; adopt scientific management practices and distinctive leadership at work. The entrepreneur has to empower his people and encourage teamwork that is creative and adventurous in what they are doing, thus realizing "from each his best ability". With these principles at heart, the ailing enterprise can then be revived!

Note: At a later time, Lee and his successor made mistakes that cost the company losses.

Case Study 2: Reaction To The Needs Of Society, Creation Of Property Business Success

By the age of 40, the Hong Kong entrepreneur Henry Fok Ying Tung had already become a shipping magnate and a millionaire. The year was 1954. He was not satisfied with his early achievements and continued to explore other business opportunities.

He established "Henry Fok Estate Limited". The company began its venture into estate development; buying over many buildings, demolishing old ones and building new ones.

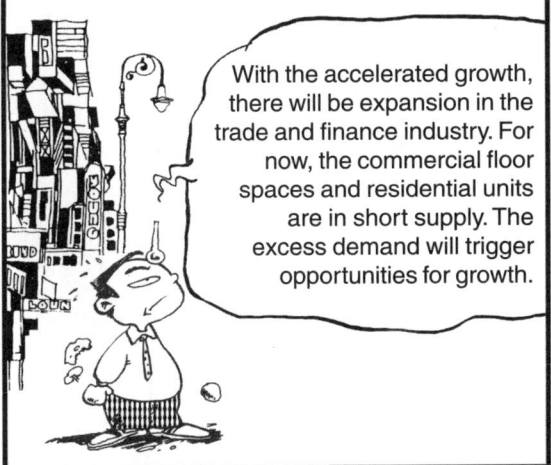

> With the accelerated growth, there will be expansion in the trade and finance industry. For now, the commercial floor spaces and residential units are in short supply. The excess demand will trigger opportunities for growth.

> I am going into the property and estate market to look for a new breakthrough in my career.

Henry Fok Estate Limited

Henry Fok's business venture was not smooth. The property prices in Hong Kong plummeted in 1967. The newly-built Star House Building was short of tenants and had to be sold to British buyers. Henry Fok lost HKD 30 million in that deal. This loss made him realize the pain of defeat but also made him more determined to succeed.

> It is necessary to be creative to open up new avenues!!

The current Hong Kong property regulations only permit the rich to buy properties. The buyer needs to pay hundreds of thousands as lump sum payment just to seal a deal. He also must pay the full sum to get his property. There must be flexibility in the system to boost the property market.

Case Study 3: Timely Capture Of The Business Opportunity

The railways and bridge infrastructures in the 1860s were all cast from steel. This led to many accidents. Andrew Carnegie was a railway worker and was deeply troubled about these accidents.

"There is a new metallurgy developed in Europe. I am seeing a revolutionary material on its debut. If I can commercialize the innovation, there will be many business opportunities! I am going to put in all my capital to build a steel mill!"

"This situation must change!"

One day, he heard of a new metallurgy innovation.

There were some reservations from his younger brother.

"All our money? That is too risky!"

"I strongly believe that this is THE opportunity! It is worth the risk."

Carnegie tried all ways to look for the necessary capital. He finally managed to raise the required capital but to his dismay, the land owner of the steel mill wanted to raise the lease price. Carnegie was a determined man and nothing could change his decision.

"I believe that this should be the price per acre."

"Fine! I will buy it!"

The steel mill was finally built. The market for his steel business was huge and the profitability doubled every year; two million, five million, ten million. By 1890, the profitability for the steel mill was USD 40 million.

Never lose sight of a timely business opportunity. Being timely and accurate are the necessary business capabilities of an entrepreneur.

Case Study 4: What's Next?
The Crossroads For Enterprise Transformation

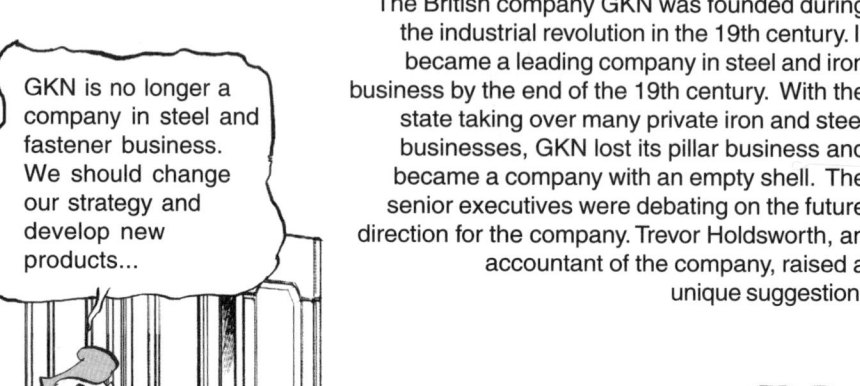

The British company GKN was founded during the industrial revolution in the 19th century. It became a leading company in steel and iron business by the end of the 19th century. With the state taking over many private iron and steel businesses, GKN lost its pillar business and became a company with an empty shell. The senior executives were debating on the future direction for the company. Trevor Holdsworth, an accountant of the company, raised a unique suggestion.

GKN is no longer a company in steel and fastener business. We should change our strategy and develop new products...

You are an accountant. What do you know about business strategies?

The company did not accept Holdsworth's suggestion and carried on with the steel and iron business.

After two short years, the steel pipe factory stopped operation and was forced out of business. The company board of directors changed their opinion. The chairman promoted Holdsworth to be the vice president.

We have just started production in our 6 million-ton steel pipe factory. To change the direction would mean all efforts will be wasted!

Holdsworth may be right!

We should give him an opportunity to try his suggestion.

The Entrepreneur
Section 2   The moral upbringing of an entrepreneur

> 将者，智、信、仁、勇、严也。
> The general has these qualities: wisdom, credibility, benevolence, courage, and discipline.
> — *Chapter: Initial Assessment* 《始计篇》
>
> 进不求名，退不避罪，唯民是保，而利于主，国之宝也。
> The general who does not advance to seek glory, or does not withdraw to avoid punishment, but cares for only the people's security and promotes the people's interests, is the nation's treasure.
> — *Chapter: The Terrain* 《地形篇》

The basic qualities of a good general are: wisdom, credibility, benevolence, courage and discipline.

A good general will not ask for glorified decoration if he wins and will not evade responsibility when he is defeated. He will faithfully guard the interests of his people and remain loyal to the country. The general is the pillar of the country.

The morals of a general, mentioned in Sunzi's Art of War, are collectively called the "Five Morals" (五德). These moral values are relevant qualities for an entrepreneur. The entrepreneur executes his strategies timely in depth and scope according to the political and economic situations. He needs to possess an acute business sense and good strategies. The entrepreneur has to remember that "credibility" is an intangible asset for accelerated growth.

The bottomline of a businessman is profitability but he must be credible and honest in his actions. By backstabbing his competitor, profiteering from consumers and capitalizing on his employees to reap profits will mean disaster for others and himself too. A good entrepreneur will always be the pioneer in the development of the nation's economy and society. He is also a well-respected philanthropist.

We study Sunzi's *Art of the War* to understand its essence and promote the "five morals". Besides the "five morals", the entrepreneur needs to have other values like, "diligence", "humbleness" and "loyalty".

Case Study 5: Be Bold In Opportune Investment

In 1992, Li Ka-Shing reckoned that the economic reform of Mainland China was full of opportunities. He believed that he should invest more aggressively in China. He immediately decided to invest in "Oriental Plaza" in Beijing. The Chinese economy showed signs of an economic overheat in 1993 and the government began to control the size of investment in China to cool down the economy. Some critics pointed out that Li Ka-Shing misjudged the Chinese economy.

Oh no! The "Oriental Plaza" investment is in trouble.

The investment environment in China is still undeveloped!

Li Ka-Shing's belief: There is no such thing as an absolutely developed investment environment. What is needed is an environment of substantial maturity. Once there is a problem coming your way, think of a solution. For development projects in Hong Kong, a building that is less than 100 metres is not considered as a skyscraper. The Oriental Plaza project is only 70 metres high, but we forgot that this is Beijing. Beijing is the capital of China and is also the ancient capital for many dynasties.

In its urban layout planning regulations, the old palace was taken as the centre of old city which all buildings must take reference from. All constructions must be in architectural harmony with the old city and the old palace. The height limit in the old city was set at 30 metres while other designated areas were set at 45 metres. The location of Oriental Plaza was within a regulated area but its height of 70 metres violated the building height regulation.

After a careful analysis, Li Ka-Shing admitted that the building project of Oriental Plaza was flawed.

The Chinese government stated clearly: Construction projects exceeding USD 100 million would need to seek approval from the central government. The construction of the Oriental Square was more than USD120 million. The city officials did not seek approval from the central government before construction. In the ensuing days after the Lunar New Year in 1995, the central government issued an injunction order to stop the construction work of the Oriental Plaza project.

Li Ka-Shing ran through his thoughts: As a matter of principle, the Chinese central government will not yield to any request. We should take the initiative to discuss with the city officials to consider design changes to the project. We need to make a press statement on the injunction by the central government on the construction.

Cheung Kong (Holdings) Limited abide to the rules and regulations of the Chinese government. All foreign investments in China are regulated by the same procedures and conditions.

The news media in Hong Kong reported on this incident.

"Cheung Kong Holdings suffers heavy losses with delay in construction and redesign of the Oriental Plaza Project!"

"The Chairman of Cheung Kong Holdings, Li Ka-Shing, is in deep woes."

What losses and woes? The property prices in mainland China are not on par with Hong Kong property prices. At Hong Kong's property peak, the price-to-cost ratio was 10:1. In China, it is the reverse. We will continue with our golf sessions and meetings. Let's not be unduly worried about it.

The shareholders of Cheung Kong Holdings were buoyed by the immense show-of-confidence in Li Ka-Shing. The share price of Cheung Kong Holdings was the least affected by the incident.

In June 1996, the Oriental Plaza obtained approval from the central government and the construction was completed in October 1999. The opening of Oriental Plaza was a victorious moment for Li Ka-Shing. He was correct in seizing the right moment and overcoming difficulties to become one of the first few foreign businessmen to venture into the Chinese market.

Risks exist for investment in both an undeveloped or developed market. Confidence in management direction and the capacity to overcome obstacles for a company comes from the entrepreneur's competence in making the right judgment and bold decision. An acute sense that adjusts to changes in economic and political situations is also a pre-requisite in the war of businesses.

Case Study 6: Establishing A Company While Operating In Debt

The young American entrepreneur, John D. Rockefeller, had only USD 800 when he started his business. This capital was borrowed from his father. In return, his father laid down very harsh lending conditions. This was a test of determination for his son.

As your father, I can lend you USD 1,000. However, the interest will be 100%!

Father, you are indeed KIND. I will borrow from you!

The young Rockefeller looked for his partner, Clark. For his business expansion, he once again went to his father.

Remember that the interest is 100%!

Rockefeller persevered and carried on with his business. Soon, positive results were yielded in the business venture. Unfortunately, the partnership fell apart in 1865. The company's debt then was USD 100,000, but the young Rockefeller was not to quit. At the auction of the business, Rockefeller fought hard to stay in business while Clark decided to give up.

All right. This business is yours!

I had been in debt the very day I started my small trading company. The debt situation is not frightening when the business is expanding and profit is on the rise. The main point is: do you have the capability to manage a business?

Rockefeller did not have the money to buy over the business. He went to a bank and asked for a loan of USD 725,000.

Once the entrepreneur has identified the "path-to-success" of a product, he needs to persevere and overcome all odds and difficulties along his journey.

Case Study 7: Sincerity In Customer Service

Vincent Green was an honest lottery ticket seller in Vancouver City, Canada. In February 1987, a customer Louis Barker bought USD 18 of lottery tickets.

Sir, according to the rules and regulations, you should pick the numbers However, I am honoured and glad to be of service and may you be lucky!

If the numbers are drawn, call my number and I will share 10% of the winnings with you.

The jackpot prize is USD 3.6 million!

Pal, why don't you pick a number for me?

Mr Barker, you have won. Come and claim your winnings!

A few days later, the lottery results were announced. However, Barker did not believe his good luck.

You have really won the prize!!

Green was afraid that Barker would miss the collection deadline. He gave him another phone call.

I am busy. Please stop your prank joke with me.

I am not joking. Come and claim your winnings!

That was unbelievable! You could have taken the winnings all by yourself! Why bother to call me?

Green persisted in his phone calls to Barker. The confused Barker half-believingly went to Green's lottery store. Green accepted only 10% of the winnings.

Quick! Claim your winnings!

Honesty is an important virtue for a businessman.

An entrepreneur gains trust by sincerity and credibility. Sincerity is an indispensable virtue and a source of power. It is applicable to all relationships; customers and colleagues, superiors and subordinates.

Case Study 8: Never Lose Credibility

Boss! The project cost exceeded our estimate by 7 times. If we go ahead with the project, we might land up in a bankrupt situation.

In 1953, the owner of Hyundai Construction, Chong Ju Yong, won a contract to re-build a bridge. The Korean War that had just ended resulted in extreme inflation for the South Korean economy.

Hyundai Construction spent a lot of money and ensured that the project was completed on time. The entire project nearly made the company go bankrupt.

To avoid further loss to the company, I suggest that we stop all construction!

Monetary loss is small matter, a tarnished credibility is a big issue!! I would rather be a bankrupt and see to it that we fulfil the contract.

Chong Ju Yong's credibility won him many more contracts and bigger projects. Soon, he won all four of the biggest construction projects in post-war South Korea.

Later, Chong Ju Yong won the high profile contract to construct Hangang Daegyo Bridge. This project lasted for 10 years and brought handsome profits to Hyundai. Hyundai Construction is now a leading construction firm of Korea.

Cultivating a credible image is the only way for an entrepreneur to build up his intangible asset. Chong Ju Yong knows this maxim well.

Case Study 9: Trading In The Middle Of War

In 1932, the Japanese Imperial Army invaded Shanghai. The insurance companies, on seeing the increased threat of war, imposed many conditions for underwriting insurance.

During the war, there will not be any insurance underwriting for merchant ships in the Chinese waters.

The war resulted in the drastic fall in the price of local produce in the domestic market. On the other hand, shortages of Chinese produce overseas caused an upsurge in price in foreign markets.

The main line of business of Gu Qing Ji Trading House was in the trading of domestic animal products of pig brittle, goat skin and other local produces. The owner, Gu Geng Yu, realized the difficulties ahead.

The packaging and delivery of the items into international waters will not take more than two weeks. If we are willing to bear the risk for two weeks, we can make a handsome profit. Our warehouse is located in the leased territory of Shanghai. The goat skin might not survive the air raids by the Japanese planes even if they have not deteriorated.

The goat skin will deteriorate in prolonged storage. We need to think of a solution immediately!

We need not adhere strictly to a cash-on-delivery practice for the sales. We can wait till the ship has gone into international waters. The ship takes two days to reach international waters. Payment to be made two days after the ship has departed from the habour. Within these two days, any loss or damage to the goods concerned, be it due to hijack or attack by the Japanese army, the losses will be incurred by Gu Qing Ji Trading House.

Risks and opportunities co-exist in businesses. The entrepreneur needs to have sharp eyes that see opportunities in risks and take bold actions in return for success.

Gu Geng Yu went to Shanghai to discuss the deal with his foreign trading partners.

The Entrepreneur
Section 3 Dangerous traits of an entrepreneur

> 故将有五危，必死可杀，必生可虏，忿速可侮，廉洁可辱，爱民可烦。凡此五者，将之过也，用兵之灾也。覆军杀将，必以五危，不可不察也。
>
> There are five dangerous traits of a general:
> He who is reckless can be killed.
> He who is cowardly can be captured.
> He who is quick tempered can be insulted.
> He who is moral can be shamed.
> He who is fond of the people can be worried.
> These five traits are faults in a general, and are disastrous in warfare.
> The army's destruction, and the death of the general are due to these five dangerous traits.
> They must be examined.
>
> — *Chapter: Nine Variations of Tactics* 《九变篇》

There are five dangerous traits for a general.
· Courageous but without stratagem · Action by brute force · Cowardice · Impatient for results · Overprotective of oneself and own reputation · These five weaknesses will lead to failure and they cannot be overlooked.

In Sunzi's *Art of War*, it was written: the flaws in the personality of the commanding general will dictate the outcome of the war. A general in war must be able to think logically and calmly in a chaotic situation. A muddle-headed general will lose a war.

Among the five personality deficiencies pointed out by Sunzi, two of them are unique:

(1) Protecting oneself is natural for most of us. Taking care of one's own reputation is a virtue. However, as the commanding general, an over-protective character will become a weakness for exploitation. The enemy will insult and annoy you, making you lose control of the situation, and attack while you are at your weakest.

In the three kingdom era when the Shu (蜀) and Wei (魏) countries were fighting, the brilliant strategist-premier of Shu, Zhu Ge Liang (诸葛亮) tried to agitate the general of Wei, Si Ma Yi (司马懿) by sending him women attire and a written declaration of war. The intent was to mock at him and force him to war. General Si Ma Yi realized this was a ploy and simply laughed off the harassment. The ploy of Premier Zhu Ge Liang was unsuccessful in this attempt.

(2) A general must differentiate the long-term and short-term benefits, overall or partial benefits. In a war, the enemy will use atrocious schemes on some of our people to achieve the aims of threatening, containment and harassment.

> The business arena is like a battlefield! As entrepreneurs, you will have to know what your dangerous personality traits are and which are the ones that will affect your business activities. Whether one can enter into business, one needs to analyse his character.

Case Study 10: Fallen Prey To Ego And Dismissal Of A Capable Employee

Lee Iacocca was once a salesman in Ford Corporation. For his excellent sales performance, Iacocca was promoted by Henry Ford as the General Sales Manager for Washington area. In 1972, Ford again promoted Iacocca as the president while he assumed the responsibility of chairman.

To achieve good sales for the company, you will need to successfully sell the "Ford Mustang".

We will need to develop the small engine automobiles!

The current strategic direction is fine. Why change?!

As the company's president, Iacocca had many clashes in management decisions with the chairman, Ford.

Iacocca maintained his vision in automobiles with small capacity engines. In 1973, the Arab-Israeli war ended with an oil crisis that hit the world's economy. The small capacity automobiles, which consumed less fuel, became instant hot sellers and proved to be a commercial success. The result spoke for itself. Iacocca was right in his vision.

Hmmm! What is so great about it!

That is an outright disrespect for me!

The excellent sales result brought fame and credibility to Iacocca. Iacocca was invited to deliver his speech at a seminar by the American bankers and financial analysts. His speech was well-received by the audience. The green-eyed Ford was affronted by Iacocca's good treatment at the seminar.

When one has fallen prey to ego and is overwhelmed by fame and reputation, jealousy will displace sensibility. This will lead to mistakes in decisions and regrets.

Case Study 11: Craving For Greatness And Success

The "King of Sports Car", John Delorean, decided to manufacture a high end sports car.

The sports car was christened as DMC-12. The body frame was built from stainless steel. The top speed of the car exceeded 200 km/hour. Its sleek body shape looked like a seagull. The sporty and chic look was wonderful…

Optimistic estimates put the sales figure as less than 12,000.

This is such a wonderful car. We should produce at least 20,000 of DMC-12 per year.

Delorean ignored the market analyst suggestion of the plausible sales figure.

What is similar between God and me? We are both outcasts by traditionalists. History proves it is always the outcasts that will make history.

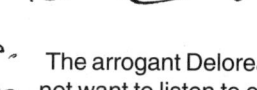

The arrogant Delorean did not want to listen to others.

Delorean began mass producing DMC-12. The annual sales figure was only 5,500 cars.

The price is too expensive!

The maintenance is troublesome!

With the huge inventory in the car garage, Delorean ran into a cash flow problem. He obstinately refused to change his management and sales strategy. An arrogant person, Delorean, started to trade in narcotics that brought high returns to pay off his company's mounting cash flow problem. On 29 September 1982, Delorean was caught red-handed by FBI in a drug transaction.

Sheer arrogance and boorish acts from incapacity for a calm analysis are shortcomings that lead directly to failure in competition. The entrepreneur needs to have the capacity to reflect upon the situation and maintain calmness in harsh conditions. Only then, can he turn adversity to triumph.

Case Study 12: Downfall That Stems From Indulges In Self-Admiration

Wang Computers was once the most successful computer company in Corporate America.
Dr Wang tirelessly rolled out new products for over 10 years, especially minicomputers and heralded in a new era in office automation.

You are now one of the five richest men in the United States of America.

The technology advancement in office automation quickly outmoded related products in the industry. However, the drive for innovation in Wang Computers remained stagnant.

The personal computer market is flourishing. IBM and other makers have developed new products and software. If we still remain where we are…

We must believe in our technology. Stay firm in the minicomputer market.

IBM personal computers have become the mainstream product for many users. Other companies are making their products compatible with IBM computer architecture platform…

We have faith in our product design!

Wang was reluctant to accept the superiority of his competitors' products and failed to learn from them. Making use of his power as the major shareholder in the company, the senior Wang made his son, Wang Lie, the company's president. The entire company was in despair by the announcement. The younger Wang could not turn the company around.

Shortcomings in a person's character such as conceit, lack of forethought and complacency are the death-wounds for a company's development. The managers from various departments will have a better understanding of the underlying problems within the organization. If the leader is not receptive to suggestions but act in his own way, he will lose people's confidence. The company will thus be driven into the abyss of bankruptcy.

Chapter 2
Managing the Employees

Section 1 **Empowerment**

Section 2 **The way of employment, administration and operation**

Section 3 **Harmonious communication**

Managing the Employees
Section 1　Empowerment

> 将能而君不御者胜。
> One whose general is able and is not interfered by the ruler will be victorious.
> 　　　　　　　　　　— *Chapter: Attack by Stratagem* 《谋攻篇》
>
> 君之所以患于军者三：不知军之不可以进而谓之进，不知军之不可以退而谓之退，是谓縻军；不知三军之事而同三军之政，则军士惑矣；不知三军之权而同三军之任，则军士疑矣。三军既惑且疑，则诸侯之难至矣。是谓乱军引胜。
>
> There are three ways the ruler can bring trouble to the army:
> To order an advance when not realizing the army is in no position to advance, or to order a withdrawal when not realizing the army is in no position to withdraw.
> This is called enmeshing the army.
> By not knowing the army's matters, and administering the army in the same way as administering civil matters, the officers and troops will be confused.
> By not knowing the army's calculations, and taking command of the army, the officers and troops will be hesitant.
> When the army is confused and hesitant, the neighboring rulers will take advantage.
> This is called a confused and hesitant army leading another to victory.
> 　　　　　　　　　　— *Chapter: Attack by Stratagem* 《谋攻篇》

　　A ruler who does not interfere and seek to control a capable general will bring victory. A ruler who does not know the position and status of an army but order for an attack or retreat; a ruler who is not involved in the administration of the army and wants to interfere with the internal affairs; a ruler who does not know the command and control of the army decides to make his command heard. The above are ways that the ruler can create confusion within an army and thus lead to attack by enemies and ultimate defeat.

　　In the feudal states of Spring-Autumn era (770BC to 576 BC), Sunzi already emphasized the need for the ruler to empower the military control of the generals. He believed that there must be clear demarcation of responsibilities among the ranks. This was quite revolutionary at that time. If the ruler, who is the supreme leader, empowers his subordinates there is no reason for anyone to cling on to absolute power. This is a clear show of belief and principle.

　　Empowerment is a sophisticated quality in leadership. The most capable of all leaders will not be able to take care of everything. The war is always complex and chaotic. The commander needs to react according to the situation. An intelligent superior will trust his subordinate, allowing him the space to exercise his initiative and creativity.

　　In the corporate world, especially the large companies, managing the company itself is an issue of huge complexity. To fulfil the responsibilities of an entrepreneur is no small feat. Excessive interference will
(1) divert the entrepreneur attention from more important matters.
(2) make the subordinate feel redundant, thus losing the sense of responsibility and eagerness.

Case Study 13: Empowering Management, Reversing Surpluses From Deficit

The management decisions of the Scandinavian Airlines had always been undertaken fully by the general manager. This greatly reduced the management efficiency of the company.

Every employee's recruitment will have to be reviewed by me.

I am the fleet maintenance manager. Even a small operational issue of getting a maintenance truck needs to get approval?!

The company needs an aircraft engineer and it takes three months for an approval!

By 1981, the company's loss widened to USD 8 million. To improve the situation, the airlines employed Jan Carlson as the new general manager. Carlson was a strong believer of empowerment in management.

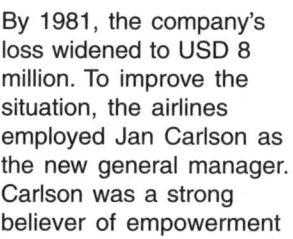

From now on, the company will be broken up into business subunits, each with its own profit and loss accountability. Every regional manager will be an empowered business owner. You can decide the weekly flight number and schedule between two cities.

You will have the freedom to seek out new businesses. You can expand beyond the current business scope of Scandinavian Airlines.

With the empowerment given by Carlson, the various departments in the company were rejuvenated and buzzing with activities.

The Engineering Department used to focus on internal maintenance requests. It actively seeks out maintenance contracts from other airlines and the results are encouraging.

The European Civil Aviation Unit leased out a few aircraft and returned good profit from the leasing agreement.

With management empowerment and division of authority, the departments can successfully "practise what the managers preach". They will be liable for their actions. Empowerment prevents the sense of helplessness experienced by managers not given the real authority. Empowerment leads to higher efficacy in management and economic returns.

Case Study 14: "Let Loose. Allow Him The Way!"

The founders of Cisco, Len Bosack and Sandy Lerner, a husband-and-wife team, were professors in Stanford University. In 1984 they established Cisco Systems, a technology company to market their unique innovation. After three years of untiring efforts, Cisco bought its office building and moved in.

The "routers" and "interchanges" of our company are quoted by the info-comm industry as the necessary "spade" and "shovel" for data mining on the internet. These are the best high-end products currently available in the market.

The rapid development of the network industry led to fierce competition. Although Cisco was operating in the hi-tech business, the management model was still very much run as a family business.

We should let go of our clinch on management. Allow the experts to do the job.

In the winter of 1988, the Bosacks employed John P. Morgridge to head the company.

We will leave the management of the company to you and concentrate on our forte in R&D work.

By 1994, the sales surged and the profitability increased by 200 times, reaching a figure of USD 323 million. Cisco had, by then, developed into the most prominent enterprise in America's network business.

The Bosacks' sharp sense of the technological developments made them realize that Morgridge's management philosophy was outdated in the internet era.

Morgridge had been an important player in the initial stage of Cisco development. However, his management style seemed to run behind the times these days.

The characteristic of info-comm business is that the company needs to constantly develop new products. Any slack in development effort will lead to losing of market share and being squeezed out of business.

After a detailed corporate analysis, the board of directors of Cisco selected John T. Chambers as the president and chief executive officer.

The average lifespan of a dog is 10 years and that is 1/7 the lifespan of man. The "dog years" in internet age requires us to achieve seven years of results from one year's effort.

Our management philosophy is: To accelerate development to achieve multiplier effect in growth.

Chambers introduced the "dog years" or "internet year" analogy to the company the moment he took over as CEO.

Chambers looked for innovation and devised a "win-win" sales strategy. Cisco joined forces with other high-tech companies like Intel and Microsoft to form a global strategic sales alliance.

Our routers have already connected 85% of the internet. Now is the time for us to move the products both upstream and downstream.

Practice the maxim "Non-interference by the ruler on his capable generals"! The "ruler" empowered the "generals". Allow for flexibility to appoint, decide and manage the finances by the "generals". The "ruler" can thus be burden-free. Similarly, with the trust in them, the "generals" can command with confidence and achieve success.
"Let Loose, Allow him the Way!"

Case Study 15: With Trust Comes The Power

Yoshiaki Tsutsumi was the chairman of the Japanese Conglomerate Seibu Group. He relied on a unique management philosophy to gain successes. His recruitment belief was most outstanding. Once, Tsutsumi wanted to choose a manager to lead the Izu-Hakone Railway line subsidiary.

"These are two business professionals whom we think are the suitable candidates."

"I think Koumura is a suitable candidate."

"Koumura is just a junior employee."

"Mr Tsutsumi, I admire you and your management beliefs. I do not think I am a good candidate for promotion."

"I understand that you are worried the other two business managers will not give you their support. Let your mind be at ease. I trust that you can do it. If there is any issue related to the Izu-Hakone line, I will listen to your input."

As expected, the two business managers were not co-operative. Six months had passed and the two business managers had no way of directly reporting to Tsutsumi. The executive authority of Koumura had finally been set.

In October 1978, Seibu Group bought a baseball team. The team was reorganized to be known as the Seibu Lions.

> This team is no good. You must change the coach!

> There are many reasons why the team is not performing. I do not think that the coach is fully responsible. He should stay with the post. It does not matter when the championship is ours, as long as it becomes reality in my life time.

The faith Tsutsumi had was a strong encouragement for the team coach, Rikuo Nemoto. In the third year under his coaching, the Seibu Lions leaped from the last position to the fourth position in the Japanese Baseball Championship. It became the league champion in 1982 and 1983.

> To promote a management executive, we must make an overall study of his work performance, conduct and family life; and that would include his family members. With this understanding then we make a decision. Once a decision is finalized, we must stand by it and give the person the necessary trust and empowerment.

> **Managing an enterprise is analogous to captaining a ship. If the captain stands on the land and gives his orders, that will not do. What you need is to build a top grade ship and select a good captain. With your destination set, the good captain will help you reach the destination.**

Case Study 16: Trust The Employed, Employ The Trustworthy

There were 7,000 employees and 13 deputy shipyard managers in Tianjin Xin Gang Shipyard. The areas of responsibility were not clearly defined and productivity suffered. The shipyard plant manager, Wang Ye Zhen, was adamant to make changes to the current management practice. He started a new reporting system that was based on hierarchy and chain reporting. For routine work, some ground rules were set. A superior will not bypass his direct subordinate to give instructions to the lower level; he, however, is allowed to check on the lower levels. The lower level will not ask for instructions two levels up but is allowed to feedback and make suggestions to higher levels.

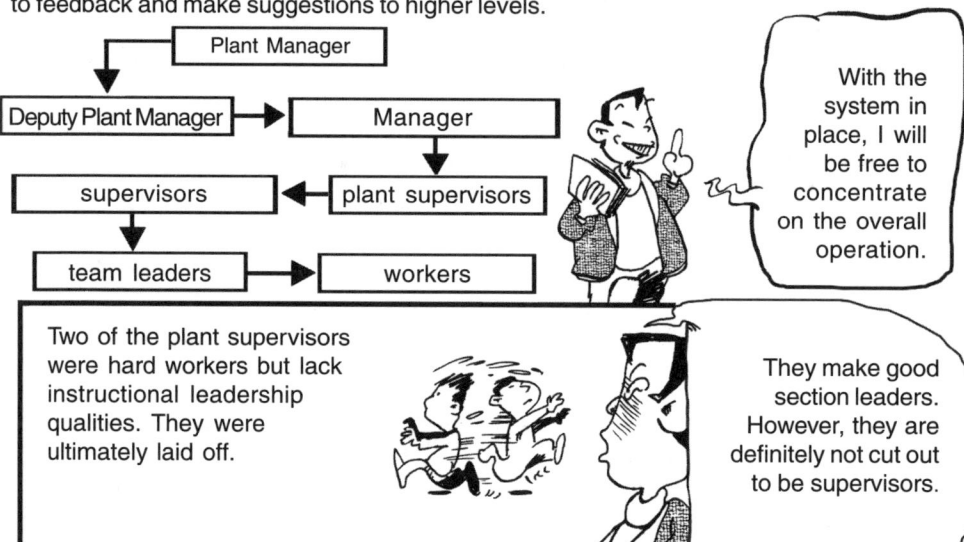

"With the system in place, I will be free to concentrate on the overall operation."

Two of the plant supervisors were hard workers but lack instructional leadership qualities. They were ultimately laid off.

"They make good section leaders. However, they are definitely not cut out to be supervisors."

If the superior is to endlessly interfere with his subordinate's work, this will only add on more work for himself and lower the leadership development opportunity for his subordinates. The overall productivity of the company will also suffer.

"After the revamp of the management system, the shipyard was systematic and orderly in executing its work processes. It was selected as one of the top 10 model enterprises in management excellence in China."

An incapable executive should not be deployed. However, once he is designated with the job scope, trust must be given to allow him the greatest autonomy in work.

Managing the Employees
Section 2 The way of employment, administration and operation

> 故令之以文，齐之以武，是谓必取。
> He commands them by benevolence, and unifies them by discipline. This is called certain victory.
>
> *— Chapter: On the March* 《行军篇》

To be benevolent is to educate and influence the men with the correct morals. To use discipline is to be strict in setting rules and regulations to achieve unified actions. Only disciplined soldiers are able to win a battle.

Sunzi believed: Before the men respect his commanders, severe punishment will lead to rebellion. Even when respect has been established, without the necessary discipline, the army will not win a war.

Sunzi advocated that the commanders must persistently instill the men with correct morals. At the same time, discipline must be enforced to unify the troops.

An entrepreneur must learn the techniques of emotional deposit. Only one who touches the heart of others is able to command lasting loyalty. The topics of how to motivate employees and improve productivity have been widely discussed by management academics and practitioners. Grinding these topics to its essence, the question of how to reward and penalize depends on the company state of affairs and its conditions. To inspire the employees' initiative and enthusiasm is what Sunzi means by the way of Civil and Military (文武之道).

Case Study 17: Unique Training And Effective Management

PepsiCo is the second largest soft drink company. In 1989, its sales figure was USD 15.4 billion. PepsiCo has its unique human resource practices. Former PepsiCo CEO Wayne Calloway emphasized on human resources. He specially established a Young Executives Training Centre.

This is the best system to transform young executives into capable managers. We brought in the young rookies and teach them to fly in formation.

The standards in training are stringent and require the trainees to do at least 60 hours of work per week. To deal with emergencies, the trainees must learn to work on weekends too. The trainees are taught how to deal with risks, not to rely too much on writing memos and holding meetings. Being decisive is a quality of an entrepreneur.

For decisions on big issues, it should be laid out as an intelligent discussion and not a personal attack.

If an issue can be settled by a phone call, there's no need to write memos and discuss in meetings.

Having been trained to deal with risks will make the managers stronger and more enterprising. If you have not made a mistake in management, chances are, you have not tried hard enough in businesses.

Wayne Calloway spent two months to review more than 550 of his top senior executives.

At each winter season, PepsiCo conducts a performance review of its 20,000 employees. The performance of the employees is classified into four categories. Those employees who fall into the last category will be disqualified. The third category will need continuous training. The second category will get a chance to be promoted but have to wait for a suitable position. Employees whose reviews are in the first category are destined for immediate promotion.

The employees who are classified in the lowest category in performance for two consecutive years will be shown the exit.

PepsiCo designed many reward programmes to make the employees understand that excellent managerial staff will be well rewarded.

Middle and upper management staff are allowed to stay in first-class hotels on business trips.

The upper management staff will have an annual wage of USD 96,000 to USD 144,000, bonus, stock options and other additional incentives.

They may choose to sit in the first-class cabin.

Staying in first-class hotels and travelling in first-class cabins is a form of psychology rewards. This symbolizes that we are a first-class company with top-class employees.

Rewarding the employees with excellent packages is more economical and efficient than instituting a big framework to supervise the organization.

Case Study 18: Inspiration And Its Effect

Lincoln Electrics was established more than 100 years ago and provides advanced welding and cutting technologies to the world's major industries. Its major customers are in the steel, oil and construction industries which are subjected to fluctuations in business cycles. Lincoln Electrics, however was not affected by the cyclical effect but remained strong in its figures. This stellar performance has a direct relationship with the company's unique human resource management and rewards system.

The company's reward system first started in 1934. Here is how the system works:
(1) The employees are not given a basic salary but a formulated salary. Each job requirement will have its corresponding formulated salary. An employee's salary = employee's production value + bonus from the company's profit.

(2) Minimize the non-productive expenses relative to the product.

There is no dispute on whether one works more or less.

No dental benefits. No holiday subsidies. No sick leave or personal leave.

Till now, the last dismissal of an employee in Lincoln Electrics took place more than 30 years ago.

A devoted employee will be assured of a stable job. (3) Employees who stayed on with the company for more than two years will get a basic assurance that there will be no dismissal. The company adopted a very stringent guideline on dismissal. Dismissal of an employee based on poor business performance is not allowed. Half a year's notice needs to be given for employees to be laid off.

A no-retrenchment policy is a risky promise for a company. However, Lincoln Electrics stood firm in this practice, even in a business downturn.

We have no intent to lay off any of our employees. We will make use of this opportunity to provide training for some of the employees. Some employees will be redeployed to improve the sales while others will be assigned for maintenance work.

USD 4.5 million

USD 2.2 million

In 1982, the company's revenue decreased by 50% due to poorer overall economy.

As the leader of its industry, the sales figure at Lincoln Electrics has always been stable. It has a cash reserve of USD 370 million and is debt-free.

The factory in Lincoln retains its early look of the 50s when it was built. The walls are green and looked dull. The factory area also comes with no air condition. During the peak seasons, the employees will have to work additional hours.

Every company has its own unique ways to manage and that depends on its requirements and desired results. There are some that seem to be outmoded and are disregarded. However, they may have given effective results. Lincoln Electrics is one such company. Linking the three elements of productivity, rewards and employment security together may seem unusual to some but it sure works for others.

Case Study 19: Brainstorming For Ideas, Transforming Failure To Success

In 1939, Eugene Thurnel bought a wire factory and named it "North Coast Label Company".

After production began, Thurnel put in all his efforts but a business crisis still loomed.

This is a small company with six employees and four machines. If any of the machines were to break down, I will be losing money.

We need to automate the production line but we are short of capital. We can sell the company but no one will want it. We will have to close down if this carries on!

Why not get everyone to think what can we do?

From today onwards, we will have to stop production. I hope that you will not leave after what I have just said. I will give you the day's pay. I need all your wisdom to think of a way to save this factory! Please write down your suggestions.

Look for a cheaper alternative material might be a solution…

I believe that there are more solutions to a problem. Let's not restrict ourselves to think of only automation…

Thurnel received many encouraging suggestions and ideas.

If automation is not our way forward, we can look for other means of cost-cutting.

Right!! The current wire labels are printed on aluminum which is expensive. If we can find an alternative base material that is both water and fire resistant to print on, our problem will be solved!

Thurnel was elated. He went in search of such a material with the correct toughness. He finally found a material that was tough enough and which can be used as a good base material by applying a layer of latex.

This new material has greatly reduced the cost of production. We can reduce the selling price to only two-third of the aluminum labels. I will get this material patented.

Thurnel obtained a five-year patent. In this period, he expanded the factory to three times its original size and adopted full automation for production.

Make use of "Crisis Management" to motivate the employees and instill their sense of responsibility in them. Have trust in the employees and brainstorm for winning ideas to work together. This can transform the company from failure to success.

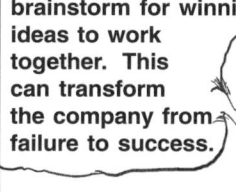

Managing the Employees
Section 3 Harmonious communication

> 故善用兵者，譬如率然。率然者，常山之蛇也。击其首则尾至，击其尾则首至，击其中则首尾俱至。敢问兵可使如率然乎？曰可。夫吴人与越人相恶也，当其同舟而济而遇风，其相救也如左右手。
> Those skilled in warfare are like the shuairan.
> The shuairan is a serpent on Mount Chang.
> If you strike its head, its tail attacks;
> if you strike its tail, its head attacks;
> if you strike its mid section, both the head and tail attack.
> Ask: Can forces be made like the shuairan?
> I say: They can.
> The men of Wu and Yue hated one another; however, encountering severe winds when crossing a river on the same boat, they assisted each other like left and right hands.
> — *Chapter: Nine Types of Strategic Grounds* 《九地篇》
>
> 故善用兵者，携手若使一人，不得已也。
> One who is skilled in warfare leads them by the hand like they are one person.
> — *Chapter: Nine Types of Strategic Grounds* 《九地篇》

Shuairan(率然) was said to be a type of serpent in Chang Shan(常山). If you hit it on its head, the tail will strike back. If you hit it on its tail, the head will strike back. Hitting at the mid-section, both the head and the tail will strike back. Hence, can the strategy be deployed to such effectiveness? Definitely it can. Look, the Wu and Yue are sworn enemies but when they were in the same boat, out in a stormy weather, they came to each other's help, just like a pair of hands.

A good strategist will be able to mobilize his army like a human exercising his four limbs. Harmonization is the process that an entrepreneur organizes his employees for their capability, benefits, psychology and productivity to achieve the organizational aims. An entrepreneur can only exercise leadership and control over the company through effective harmonization.

The productivity and efficiency of a company, the co-operation among its employees depend upon the harmony in the organization. It is the responsibility of the entrepreneur to make use of the knack of harmony to inspire his employees to form a heart-and-soul team that weathers the rough business environment.

Communication is a process that comes after the harmonization of each department and members. Communication is also a means for the entrepreneur to establish a harmonious relationship in the company. To make it more distinct, sufficient communication will lead to harmony; and a harmonious environment will lead to freedom in communication.

Case Study 20: One-Day Plant Manager Programme

In March 1983, a Korean company that specialized in producing paper wipers implemented a "One-day Plant Manager" programme. The management hoped that the programme could give its employees the experience of managing an enterprise.

Every Wednesday, one of the line employees would take on the plant manager's role in administering the daily operations.

The plant-manager-in-representation would begin work at 9 am sharp. His responsibility for the day was to accompany the actual plant manager as he made his visits to the various departments. He would have the authority to endorse on the documents for the day.

I am the manager today!

I need to listen to the briefings by the department supervisors and understand the daily operation issues.

The suggestions I make will be documented in the company's journal and circulated for reading by other employees.

I will get to see the department supervisors' reports before they are circulated for approval by the plant manager. The plant manager will listen to my suggestions before he makes his decision.

Every department supervisor has to improve work processes with my suggestions. The improvement outcome will be reviewed at the management meeting. If the improvement is satisfactory, the work improvement activity can be closed.

This programme helped the participants cultivate a greater sense of belonging to the organization.

In the past, when the plant manager spoke of "co-operation" and "cost-cutting", I would not have understood. Now I understand and am convinced about it.

If there is another chance to be the plant-manager-in-representation, I will do it better. However, the job of the plant manager is definitely not easy. Only those participants who have experienced the programme will understand.

"One-day Plant Manager" programme reaped positive results after one year of successful implementation. The suggestions that came out from this programme reduced the production cost by USD 2 million.

The USD 2 million saved will be distributed as bonuses for all employees.

Under specific conditions and environment, create positive influence on each employee. This will inspire their initiative and develop the potential of every employee. The cohesiveness created will also propel the company to greater heights.

Case Study 21: Maintaining The Co-operation And Trust Between Entrepreneur And Employees

American entrepreneur, J. Paul Getty, started his oil company at the age of 24. He often worked and ate together with his workers at the oil field.

Boss! We have faith in you.

Forget about this site. You will never be able get oil out of here. Not for a million years!

Paul leased an oil field in California at a very low rental fee. Though the rental was low, the mining at the field was difficult. The road, or more correctly, the 400-feet pathway leading to the oil field was only 4-feet wide. There was no way for trucks to bring supplies into the mining area. Many of his business associates advised him to give up on this oil field.

Guys, do we want to give up on this oil field?

Boss. Let's survey the area. We might find a solution.

At the work area, Paul and his workers discussed on the possible solutions to overcome the odds. A solution finally struck.

We can make use of small drilling tools.

We can lay a smaller track and make use of small trailers to move the supplies and equipment.

The employees' loyalty and sincere suggestions are the positive outcomes of mutual trust and respect between the entrepreneur and employees.

Case Study 22: "The Three Elements" Of Management

In 1982, the group profit of ICI dropped by 23% and reached a low of 259 million pounds. The group chairman, Sir Harvey Jones, initiated the "Three Elements" of management to improve communication and foster a harmonious work environment.

Firstly, in the face of adversity, the senior management should understand that their behaviour and action will have an impact on the employees' psychology. Hence, the senior management must maintain a buoyant and confident mood. Once, Sir Harvey attended a sales meeting and addressed the people at the meeting. The employees were confounded by his action and began speculating.

Secondly, develop an easy feedback channel for communication and opinions. Every employee would have access to the chairman to express their grievances. However, the grievances must be accompanied by suggestions for improvement.

Thirdly, expand the scope of all employees and invigorate their enthusiasm. Instead of making an employee feel left out, give the right pressure for them to actively participate.

This is the benefit of a transformation in management belief. Enterprise management needs leveraging: Leverage on the capability of each level of the organization, leverage on the communication means, and importantly, enhance communication and co-operation with employees.

Chapter 3
Strategy for Company Talents

Section 1   Knowing and deploying talents

Section 2   Improving the quality of employees and training for talents

Section 3   Sincerity towards employees

Strategy for Company Talents
Section 1　Knowing and Deploying Talents

> 将听吾计，用之必胜，留之；将不听吾计，用之必败，去之。
> A general who listens to my calculations, and uses them, will surely be victorious, keep him;
> A general who does not listen to my calculations, and does not use them, will surely be defeated, remove him.
> — *Chapter: Initial Assessment* 《始计篇》
>
> 故善战者，求之于势，不责于人。故能择人而任势。
> Those skilled in warfare seek victory through force and do not require too much from individuals.
> Therefore, they are able to select the right men and exploit force
> — *Chapter: Use of Military Momentum* 《兵势篇》

A general who is willing to listen to suggestions is to be kept to help win a war. A leader who is not willing to listen to suggestions will be taken out as he will lead a losing battle.

A good commander is one who knows how to capitalize an advantageous condition. Only discerning commanders should be deployed to lead the army.

Sunzi emphasized in *The Art of War*: Correct use of a talent will decide the outcome of a battle. A building is not supported by a single pillar but the overall foundation and all existing building knowledge. To be successful in his career, one needs to make good use of talented people.

This same emphasis can be seen in the management study of today. Human talent is the most important of all resources. Hence, how do we tap the potential of each individual to the fullest? What kind of management system will be conducive for talents to perform? These are questions that entrepreneurs need to answer.

The entrepreneurs must realize that attracting the best talents is the key to success in a competitive business. A company will need different talents at various stages of its development.

At the startup, what gets done is dependent on loyal and hardworking talents. Once the business is matured and in a sustaining stage, the talents need to be motivated and creative to propel the business to the next stage of excellence.

Case Study 23: Selecting The Right Talents

Firestone Tyre and Rubber Company began with only a few employees and was housed in an old factory. The founder, Harvey S. Firestone, believed that to expand his business, he would need to look for a new rubber tyre that is less stiff. To assist his business expansion, Firestone was always looking for the right talent to hire. One day, he met a drunkard in a pub.

"Bartender! Give me another glass!"

"Ha! Ha! He is comical."

"His name is Lautner, a drunkard."

"He has a peculiar temper."

"He is an inventor with many weird inventions."

"He knows his chemistry well!"

Once Firestone Sr. decided that Lautner was the talent he was looking for, he paid him many visits and invited him to join his company. His invitations were all rejected. Firestone did not give up.

Lautner was finally touched by Firestone's sincerity.

"I see the sincerity in you. I promise to help you succeed in your business."

Competition between companies is a competition for talents. The ability to select and appoint talents is important for a manager. A correctly selected talent can bring refreshing ideas into the company and greater achievements.

Case Study 24: Appointing Talented Individual, Growing The Company

Yamashita Toshihiko was a young executive in Sony. He was discovered as a talent by Matsushita Konosuke and made the general manager at the age of 39.

You are analytical in seeing the problems with our management. Do the necessary restructure at your discretion!

Yamashita's decisive management produced excellent results and he rose through the ranks. He was appointed a member within the Board of Directors by Matsushita. There were objections from some Matsushita family members but Matsushita Konosuke ignored their complaints.

Yamashita is the best talent in the company and we cannot find someone of his calibre from among our family members. We should break the rank and promote him.

In 1977, Yamashita, the 25th ranking within the board, took the helm as the President of Matsushita Corporation. Like his benefactor, Yamashita was keen to nurture young talents. He promoted 22 of his young managers to directors. In a short span of a few years, Matsushita's management was invigorated with young blood.

The financial results of Matsushita showed marked improvement in the second year after Yamashita took over. By 1983, the company's profitability was at an all-time high of Yen 189.1 billion. That was two times higher than the profit of Yen 97.6 billion when he first took over as president. Matsushita Konosuke has his distinctive way of identifying a talent. When an organization expanded, it became necessary to look for good talents and bring them into leadership position. Appointed talented individuals will rejuvenate the company and expand the growth areas for the company.

Case Study 25: The Pioneer Of Chinese Chemical Industry

In 1920, the Chinese entrepreneur Fan Xu Dong, founded Yong Li Company that manufactured alkaline. After careful selection, Hou De Pang was selected as the chief engineer.

"You have an illustrious chemical engineering doctorate from Columbia University. Not only are you knowledgeable, you also have much perseverance in your work. I am deeply impressed."

"I will produce the highest quality of alkaline."

At the starting stage, everything had to begin from ground zero. The pilot production was problematic and the visiting American technical experts were disheartened. They were ready to abandon the project. Fan Xu Dong withstood the mounting pressures and supported Hou's effort.

"The furnace is down!"

"The steel drums were halted under high temperature. What should we do?"

"Let's give up the project and return to America!"

"The pilot line has been through many trials. This is a drain on our valuable resources. The shareholders demand that Chief Engineer Hou be replaced!"

"Change the carbonic acid tower pipes!"

"Design a new distillation furnace!"

"Improve the cooling system!"

"Improve the filtration system."

Hou, in his work suit, worked day and night with his fellow workers to solve the problems.

In 1924, the company started mass production of pure alkaline in China.

At the 1926 World Expo in Philadelphia, China's Yong Li Company won the gold medallion award for its "Red Triangle" high purity alkaline product.

The whole chemical industry is founded on acidic and base substances. We need to perfect our processes to produce high quality chemicals.

Hou started to develop high purity acids. In 1937, the company finally produced China's first batch of high purity acids.

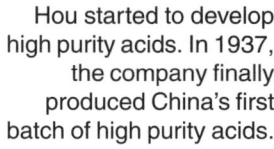

With the support of Fan Xu Dong, Hou began to develop more advanced technology in the production of alkaline.

With more than 500 experimental trials and having analyzed more than 2,000 samples, "Hou's Combinatory Alkaline Manufacturing Method" was born. This method made full use of the raw material and greatly simplified the manufacturing processes. The new technology required fewer facility resources and produced a cost-saving of more than 40%.

Correctly select an employee and correctly make use of a group of employees. This is the way to success for a company. "One who gathers the warrior flourishes, one who loses the warrior shrivels." "Winning a war belies in selecting the warriors". The leader needs to identify the "talents" and give due support and trust in them.

Strategy for Company Talents

Section 2 Improving the quality of employees and training for talents

> 主孰有道？将孰有能？天地孰得？法令孰行？兵众孰强？士卒孰练？赏罚孰明？吾以此知胜负矣。
> Which ruler has Tao?
> Which general has the ability?
> Which has gained Heaven and Ground?
> Which carried out Law and commands?
> Which army is strong?
> Which officers and soldiers are trained?
> Which reward and punish clearly?
> By means of these, I know victory and defeat!
> — *Chapter: Initial Assessment* 《始计篇》
>
> 兵非贵益多也，惟无武进，足以并力、料敌、取人而已。
> In warfare, numbers may not necessarily be an advantage; do not advance aggressively. It is enough to estimate the enemy's strength and get support from your men.
> — *Chapter: Manoeuvring* 《行军篇》

We can make strength-weaknesses analysis of competitors and ourselves from seven aspects to foretell the outcome of a battle. These aspects are:
1 Sensibility of the ruler
2 Capabilities of the commanders
3 Opportune moments
4 Chain of Commands
5 Weapon infrastructure
6 Training of troops
7 An impartial reward system

   Sunzi, in *The Art of War*, emphasized many times the role of training of troops in the battle front. A well-trained army is the result of daily training and education. We can apply this principle to the business arena. Besides selection of talents to join the company, we must also give these talents proper training to undertake their assigned tasks.

   A dynamic market place and advancement in technology gave rise to the need for corporate training. The corporate capability and its training program are closely linked. An entrepreneur needs to take his workers' training as his priority. At the same time, the training has to be supportive towards the corporate management strategies that produce a competitive market advantage. The outcomes of training and education can be evidently seen in the products and services. Only then will the corporate training programmes be meaningful.

Case Study 26: On-The-Job Training For The Talents

Formosa Plastic Group (FPG) recruits more than 500 university graduates each year. The new employees will undergo a period of probation and orientation. Before embarking on the work, there is a three-day "induction training". The training emphasis is on corporate management.

The training contents are:
1. The management philosophy of FPG and its subsidiaries.
2. The human resources, sales and marketing, production, financial and material management.
3. Production cost and sales analysis.

These training topics served as an introductory learning of the corporate management processes and values.

After the introductory classroom lessons, it will be time for an "on-the-job training". This phase of training is applicable to all newcomers regardless of qualifications and vocations. You will be assigned to the various plants of the company as part of the frontline production staff working on shift.

Besides the production shift work, we need to be involved in other logistic and maintenance assignments. This is tiring!!

We need to perform shift duties and write monthly reports that will be reviewed by our supervisors.

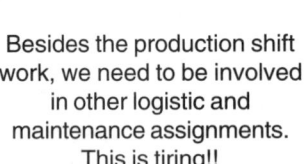

The training at shift work is very strict.

The shift work is meant as a test on the new employees' ability to take hardship. This also serves to train their determination and patience at work. For those who have failed the mark, he will not pass the probation even if he has a stellar academic result.

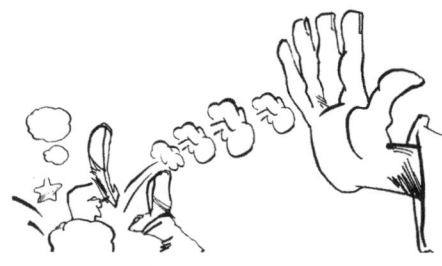

The training result is very bad!!

After the training period, there will be a test by an examiner appointed by the general manager's office. All the department supervisors are directly responsible for the outcome of the training. With a trainee's bad performance, the supervisors will also be reprimanded.

Practice
Theory

I graduated from Zhong Xing University and studied business studies as my major. I am now working in the human resource department. After the shift work and job rotation, I am able to relate the theoretical knowledge learnt in school with the actual work. With the hands-on experience, a proposed solution will not be from a theoretical basis but from a more realistic perspective. The shift work and job rotation are definitely important.

The shift work and job rotation is a system that helps new graduates to transform into managers or supervisors. This is a foundation for training the talents. These graduates will hold management or supervisory positions in some departments in future. After the training, the trainees would have experienced on-the-job work, which will prove useful for their future professional development. From both perspectives of the corporation and the new hires, this shift work and job rotation arrangement is a thing that must be encouraged.

Case Study 27: A Company And Its In-House Training Institute

The CPGroup in-house training institute was formed in 1984 to train and educate senior executives of the group. The acceptance criteria were: 1. At least five years of work with the company in production, R&D or general management. 2. Trainees must be below 45 years old. 3. The application is to be made personally by the applicant, approved by the department and endorsed by the corporate headquarters. The entrance examination tested on the trainees' practical work experience, sense of responsibility for the company's development and an interest in continual education. The yearly student enrolment size of about 100 is a strict policy for obtaining the best candidates. The trainees came from varied backgrounds but they all had a clear learning objective.

- Agricultural Farming Development and Environment Protection Studies
- Advanced Farm Products and Animal Feeds Processing and Marketing Studies

There are only two programmes offered by the institute to serve the needs of the company's production and sales. The institute has a strong academic staff of 50 professors and assistant professors. For the teaching of production technology, there are 65 trainers with both practical and teaching experience. Hence, the curriculum is practical oriented and is welcomed by the trainees.

The production facilities and sales offices worldwide provided the best training grounds and opportunities for the trainees, on top of the relevant curriculum.

The university emphasizes the practicality for the company and was founded on the ideal of lifelong learning.

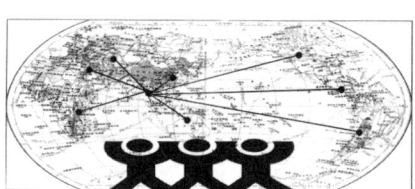

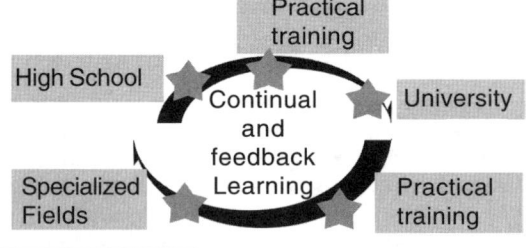

> The practical-oriented training of the university cultivated a good learning environment and is a grooming ground for hands-on senior executives.

Case Study 28: Persist In Corporate Education And Equip The Talents

Siemens of Germany was established in 1847. It has more than 400,000 employees. It is ranked among the top 20 in the best 500 corporations of the world. Siemens is the third biggest company in Germany and the world's sixth largest electronic firm. There are many reasons why Siemens has been able to survive two world wars and also the great depressions of the 1930s. The most important of these reasons is none other than the company's emphasis on education.

Siemens has never been stingy in giving training for its employees since the early days of its founding. Today, Siemens has 11 integrated training centres and more than 700 professional trainers. There are 39 training departments in 18 countries and more than 150,000 employees undergoing different kinds of training.

Opened the first "Trainee's Corner"	Started training for professional sales and marketing staff.	Established the first Factory for Training.	Established the first college by a factory.
1871	1883	1903	1906

Many of the training programmes at Siemens are at the forefront of technology. A long-term emphasis on training has established Siemens with a firm base of talents. The company relied on its illustrious group of engineers who developed the telex machines and later other products like telephones, power generators, machinery and lighting equipments, etc. Currently, Siemens maintains a strong foothold in electronics industry. In the electronic component alone, Siemens offers more than 100,000 different kinds of component products that satisfy customers' needs. The high technology products made up more than 50 percent of total sales. Siemens has made big contributions to the development of the industry and electronic era.

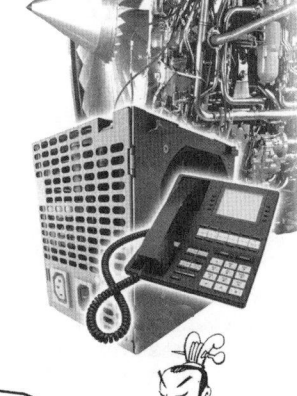

Talents are the most precious resources for a company. Training and education for these talents have profound and extensive positive effects for the company. Only through training can the company expand its market share and improve the quality of management.

Case Study 29: A Company's Investment On Training And Management

Car manufacturer, Audi, treated employees' training as an "investment" for the company's future and is generous with it. The annual training budget was 27 million German Marks. The training centres were equipped with many advanced quipment and facilities. There are robots, advanced computers, aerodynamic platform, electronic sensors, CNC machines etc.

Audi was prudent on the return-on-investment for the training. A training department was set up to look into it. The job scope of this department was to formulate the training programmes, analyse the impact of training on production downtime, trainers' employment, training facilities management. The aim was to achieve the most optimum training outcome.

To engage an external training programme producer will cost 10,000 marks per minute. In-house production costs only 1,000 mark per minute. Let's produce it ourselves.

Audi established a muti-tier training programme.

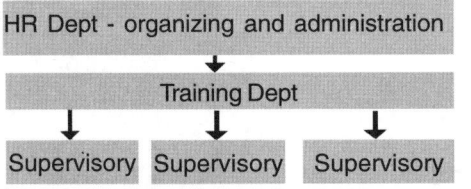

Manage and administer training activities

Every employee was loaded with work. The company supported and encouraged employees to go for training outside their work.

Training received formed part of the review criteria in salary increment and promotion.

For a business operator to strive in a competitive environment, continuous investment must be made. This will include not only the production facilities and employees' benefits, but also investment in continual employees' training. Audi realized the importance of "investment" in corporate training to maintain its competitive edge. Concurrently, it emphasized on the return-on-investment for training, prudent in training expenditure and management. These are all good corporate traits that we can learn from.

Case Study 30: Business Needs High Calibre Employees

Jiang Su Construction Company was well known in China. In the early stages, most of its workers were young native men from the farming countryside. They were hardworking but untrained in construction knowledge. When it comes to bidding for projects and speed of work, the firm prevailed. However, for projects requiring quality workmanship and technology, the firm clearly lagged behind its competitors.

"In the construction business all you need is strength and assiduousness."

"Winning the projects require strength and diligence!"

The manager at Tai Xing Province Construction Company, Hu Yao Zhong, understood the difference.

"The number of construction firms is increasing but the market size is limited. We need to change our focus from mindless expansion to improvement in the quality of our workers."

Hu tested the proficiency of his workers assigned to the company's biggest projects. The result showed that out of 14,000 workers, 2,100 failed the test.

"We will increase the salary and promote outstanding workers who pass the test!"

Hu divided his workers into teams based on three levels of proficiency. There are five criteria for proficiency:
(1) Technology
(2) Equipment capability
(3) Quality of work
(4) Safety at work
(5) Leadership

From now on, new construction projects will be given priority allocation to teams with level 1 proficiency. The rest will have to wait.

Hu emphasized on training the employees for the necessary work requirements. Vocational training programmes tapes were produced to teach the workers. Other training included supervisory and managerial skills upgrading. He also sent more than 400 employees for university education.

As a result, Tai Xing Provincial Construction Company won projects that required quality workmanship, like Beijing Exposition Hall and Shen Zhen Aviation Complex.

The market shows no mercy in choosing the winner. The company needs high calibre employees to make quality products and provide good services. Competitiveness can only be improved with high standards of quality.

Strategy for Company Talents
Section 3   Sincerity towards employees

> 卒善而养之。
> Treat the captured good soldiers well.
>
> — *Chapter: Waging War*   《作战篇》
>
> 视卒如婴儿，故可以与之赴深溪；视卒如爱子，故可与之俱死。厚而不能使，爱而不能令，乱而不能治，譬若骄子，不可用也。
> If the general is kind to the troops, but cannot use them, or if the general loves the troops, but cannot command them, or if the general does not discipline the troops, but cannot establish order, the troops are like spoiled children and are useless.
>
> — *Chapter: The Terrain*   《地形篇》

In a war, not only must we treat our men well, even for the captured enemies we should not ill treat them.

A commander that is able to treat his men well will be able to mobilize the men in a fight. The commander needs to take care of his subordinates like how he treats his children. A father who dotes on his children and does not enforce the correct discipline will spoil the children. Likewise, a commander who fails to discipline his troop will render the troop useless in the face of a battle.

In the Spring-Autumn era, it was a common practice to behead a prisoner-of-war. Sunzi advocated the need to treat the prisoner-of-war well. This notion was considered exceptional in that era of hegemonic war. It encompassed unheard civility and more importantly, the considerations from a strategic perspective. Without doubt, if one is to treat the captured enemy well, the treatment of one's own army must be better. Sunzi believed that to manage an army begins with caring for the army. The commanders can exercise his command and control through his care and relationship-building with his men. To lead an army is to lead through the heart and not through the use of force.

Human capital is the most important element for an organization. The workers form the majority of employees in an organization. A well-run and successful company is closely linked to the sense of responsibility and motivation of the majority. Treat every employee well and they will devote their effort to the company. When the employees put their heart and soul into the company, the creativity will be limitless and it brings huge profitability to the company.

Case Study 31: Treat the Employees Well, Enhance Team Spirit

Lee Kong Chian was the founder of Nam Aik Group of Companies in Singapore. He took good care of the employees' benefits. Nam Aik adopted a recruitment philosophy of lifetime employment. The employees enjoyed free medical, education and year-end bonuses. In one particular year, the company's profitability was SGD 50 million and the year-end bonus was one-fifth of the amount.

Some of the best employees were given bonuses that were equivalent to three to five years' of their salaries. However, during bad times, the previously issued bonuses would be deducted from the employees.

As the well-being of the company is closely related to the individual, the employees were passionate about their work.

There was also no grudge about overtime during holidays.

Nam Aik had long before implemented a provident fund scheme for employees.

The retirement fund was set up by money deposited by the company on behalf of the employees into a bank. The company would deduct 5% from the employee's monthly salary, on top of the 10% contributed by the company.

Nam Aik also had a "home ownership" scheme whereby the employees can borrow an interest-free loan, equivalent to three years' salaries, for the purchase of a house. The title deed would belong to the company. The repayment was by way of deduction of 50% of the yearly bonus until the principal amount had been paid up. Thereafter, the title deed would be transferred to the employee.

The onus is on the managers to take care of the workers and subordinates. The managers need to provide solutions for workers' livelihood and ease their future worries. These are the obligations that the managers owe to the development of the company and society.

Case Study 32: Attractive Incentives Draw Talents

America is the leader in the technology race and there are many reasons for its leadership position. The primal reason for its success is its policy to draw foreign talents to join its high-tech industry.

American policy-makers instituted many attractive schemes for hi-tech professionals. These schemes include high wages, bonuses, patent protection, and financial support for the professionals to work on their innovations. Once, a Swiss researcher successfully developed a system that was able to improve the image resolution of infra-red pictures from orbiting satellites. This invention attracted a worldwide attention.

Many countries approached this talented researcher with high salaries and other offerings.

We have not decided on what salary we will pay. Nonetheless, we will pay five times on top of what you are receiving now.

In the end, an American company was able to recruit the talent and bought over the entire imaging system.

A good manager is able to identify suitable talents for appointments. Worthy compensation packages will commensurate with their abilities and contributions. The talents employed can bring more fortunes and help lead the company to success. On the contrary, a wrongly appointed talent to a key position will lead not just to losses in salary and expenses, but invite disaster to the enterprise.

Case Study 33: Paying High Salaries To Attract Talent

Apple Computers was a late success in the computer business. The company's General Manager Mike Macula was a computer expert but lacked the quality of a sales person. The inadequacy stifled the development of the company.

Apple decided to hire John Scully as General Manager. The recruitment package was an annual salary and an additional USD 2 million as bonus.

An extra USD 2 million expense yearly? Is this worthwhile?

John Scully is the General Manager and a veteran in the sales and marketing of PepsiCo. He believes in quantitative management science and effectively using it in managing PepsiCo. This improved its business and narrowed the gap with its competitor, Coca Cola. At one time, the performance of Pepsi even surpassed that of Coca Cola. If we are able to make him come on board, it will be excellent.

Scully made a detailed analysis of the current management practices the moment he joined Apple. He formulated a series of sales and marketing strategies. These strategies improved Apple's sales markedly.

An entrepreneur can pay high salaries to attract talents to join the company. In competitive business, talents are precious resources. In the process of giving attractive packages for talents, one must not overpay and must identify that the candidate is indeed the right talent.

Chapter 4
The Art of Formulating Strategy

Section 1   **A winning mentality**

Section 2   **Achieving victory without a fight**

Section 3   **Thorough analysis before setting targets**

Section 4   **Technology advancement is an edge for business competition**

The Art of Formulating Strategy
Section 1   A winning mentality

> 兵者，国之大事 也。死生之地，存亡之道，不可不察也。
> Warfare is a great matter to a nation;
> it is the ground of death and of life;
> it is the way of survival and of destruction, and must be examined.
> — *Chapter: Initial Assessment* 《始计篇》

War is a matter of concern for the whole nation and requires our attention.

There was a popular quote: "Survival of the fittest". All creatures, great or small, will learn to survive in a competitive environment where resources are scarce. There is no exception for mankind too. In the past, many conflicts between countries, races or religions were concluded with wars. The outcome has always been that the winner thrived while the loser is ruined. The human civilization has reached a stage of peaceful co-existence and constructive competition. There may be a minority who believes in using force and aggression to get one's desires. The majority of people would choose peaceful trade or business co-operation as the solution to satisfying the needs. This is also the most beneficial choice for a nation.

A popular Chinese saying goes: "Shang Chang Ru Zhan Chang" (商场如战场, translated: "Doing business is like fighting a war"). It is important for the entrepreneur to realize that competition always exists as equilibrium is only transitory. Competition can make or break a business. Hence, a competitive mindset needs to be instilled in an entrepreneur. Whoever possesses the right competitive strategy will survive the competition and propel the company to the next level of development.

Case Study 34: Soft Competition

In the 1960s and 70s, Gillette was leading the race for men's shavers and accessories with two models of razor blades — "Blue Razor" and "Blue Plus". Its competitor in the business of disposable razor, BIC, introduced a new stainless steel razor blade which captured a substantial market share away from Gillette.

Gillette made a comprehensive analysis and formulated their competitive strategy. At a time of unfavourable condition, Gillette was not eager to fight back, at least not in an obvious way. Instead, Gillette spent time to re-structure and streamline the internal operations. The development team at Gillette successfully designed the world's first disposable double-blade razor, Trac II. In its advertisement pitch, Gillette proclaimed:

Trac II gives a smoother shave than its stainless steel blades predecessor, "Super Stainless".

Thereafter, it introduced an adjustable double blade razor "Atra" and other new shaving products, "Sensor" and "Contour". For each generation of razor blades, comparison of the latest features was always made to its own preceding products. This non-competitive nature of its advertising campaign was lauded by the market. Gillette re-captured 65% of the shaver market while its opponent, BIC, was beaten in this competition and lost tens of millions dollars.

In the competitive game, Gillette was never, at any time, over optimistic or self-conceited. Strategically, it seemed wilfully ignorant of its competitor while tactically, it was targeting its competitor. Business competition need not always be seen as in obvious competition especially when the market conditions are not in our favour. This situation would require a more intelligent approach to competition; what is known as "soft competition". For a business operator, this would mean to conserve the valuable resources, making minor retreat for greater advance. Gillette, while in a disadvantaged position, made concrete effort to introduce new designs and launched non-competitive advertisement campaigns. Gillette was successful in building a positive market image and good branding for the company.

Case Study 35: The Cola Market — Marketing War With No Single Winner

In 1886, pharmacist Babaton, concocted the secret recipe of Coca Cola and took the soft drink market in America by storm. Coca Cola Company, designed a 6.5-ounce drink bottle with a unique shape that was handy to carry for its consumers. A big advertising campaign was launched and echoed that the bottle was the best bottle design in history. Coca Cola sold more than 6 billion bottles of Coke in these newly designed bottles.

For 5 penny, Coca Cola offers you 6.5 ounces. Pepsi Cola offers 12 ounces!

Same price but twice the fun!

In 1939, Pepsi Cola started a price war targeting at the 6.5-ounce bottle designed by Coca Cola.

Coca Cola realized that by participating in a price war with its opponent, there would be huge difficulty in physical price adjustment for the large number of Coke drinks currently placed in the vending machines country wide. An increase in bottle capacity would mean that more than 1 billion 6.5-ounce drink bottles would have to be recalled and withdrawn from the shelves. Pepsi Cola was closing its gap with Coca Cola in this battle of colas.

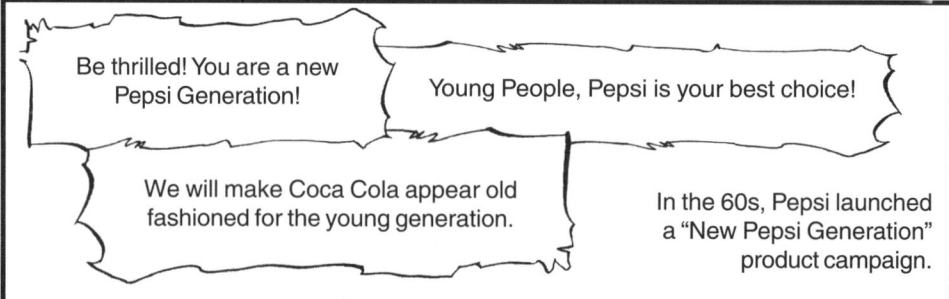

Be thrilled! You are a new Pepsi Generation!

Young People, Pepsi is your best choice!

We will make Coca Cola appear old fashioned for the young generation.

In the 60s, Pepsi launched a "New Pepsi Generation" product campaign.

In 1983, Pepsi paid USD 5 million to Michael Jackson for his endorsement of Pepsi Cola in advertisements. Thereafter, other celebrities like Lionel Richie, Tom Jones and Madonna also became the spoke-persons for Pepsi Cola. In 1985, Pepsi successfully enthroned itself as the biggest soft drink maker in the world.

Coca Cola welcomed the competition and redefined itself with many advertising campaigns. Coca Cola was the biggest soft-drink maker in the last 50 years.

In that case, hasn't Pepsi's effort been wasted? PepsiCo Chairman, Roger Enrico, had this to say.

When consumers are drawn into the advertising campaigns of Pepsi Cola and Coca Cola, it turns out to be a win-win situation. A prolonged marketing campaign creates a lasting interest in colas.

In market competition, there is no way to achieve a sure win. There is no need for that too. The creative ideas from the on-going competition will enhance the product design and inject new consumers' interest in the products. Naturally, the total market expands. Under this competitive environment, there is no single victor. Everyone is a winner.

Case Study 36: Businesses In Japan Bolstered The Economy

Japan has a small land area of 370,000 square kilometres. This land area is only 0.07% of the world's total land masses. The limited arable land is not enough to produce food sufficient for the entire population. Natural resources are scarce and it needs to rely on imports. The Japanese import: 99% of oil, 67% of coal, 82% of natural gas, 98% of iron ore and 94% of bronze. After the Second World War, the Japanese economy was at the brink of a collapse. The per capita income was USD 17. The only way to re-build their nation was to concentrate on business activities and economic development. The whole nation was supportive and rallied behind the business activities.

The Japanese products in the earlier days were low in quality. They could hardly break into the competitive Western markets. These products could only capture the lower tier markets of Asia, Africa and Latin-America where competition was low. Their products entered into the Western markets only after the technology has matured and the quality improved.

Marked improvement in the quality of Japanese products followed. The American businesses were still in the old paradigm that Japanese goods were inferior and dismissed them as potential competition. However, to their surprise, the Japanese goods proved to be value-for-money and appealed to consumers. After the 1970s, Japanese-made products dominated 70% of the colour television market and 90% of the video recorder market. Japan was also the major exporter for more than 12 other electronic products. Japan emerged as the world's second largest economy.

The rise of the Japanese economy was the consequence of dynamic competition among its local enterprises. The competitive edge of the Japanese companies was a closely knitted management. A closely knitted management was the result of the loyalty and teamwork of the employees. These qualities owed their basis to a pro-business and pro-economy attitude of post-war Japan.

Case Study 37: Understanding And Fulfilling The Consumers' Needs

In the 1950s, the fishery industry in Shikoku, Japan, consisted mainly of family-run fishing fleet. The productivity was low. The fishermen longed for an inexpensive and small-tonnage fishing trawler. Tsubouchi Toshio saw the opportunity in this niche market and bought the defunct Kurushima Dockyard and renamed it as Shin Kurushima Dockyard.

I want to create my business in the small-tonnage trawlers market which big companies like Mitsui and Mitsubishi have neglected.

The regulation for building trawlers with a gross weight of more than 500 tons was stringent and required submission of many documents. To work around the restriction, Tsubouchi decided to build trawlers less than 499 tons. The smaller trawlers would also satisfy the need of the fishermen in Shikoku.

499 tons.

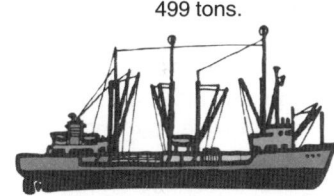

To help the honest but cash-strapped fishermen, Tsubouchi adopted a sales strategy that allowed hire purchase. He aggressively promoted the trawlers of Shin Kurushima Dockyard to the fishermen in the period when they were back for New Year.

You can pay for the new trawler in installments.

More businesses came in after the fishermen realized their economic benefits with the new trawlers.

Tsubouchi helped to expand the fishery industry in Shikoku. Likewise, the industry had also supported the growth of Kurushima fishing trawlers. In just eight years, Kurushima became the fifth largest ship building company in Japan.

The Art of Formulating Strategy
Section 2   Achieving victory without a fight

> 善用兵者，屈人之兵而非战也，拔人之城而非攻也，毁人之国而非久也，必以全争于天下，故兵不顿而利可全，此谋攻之法也。
> One who is skilled in warfare principles subdues the enemy without doing battle, takes the enemy's walled city without attacking, and overthrows the enemy quickly, without protracted warfare.
> His aim must be to take All-Under-Heaven intact.
> Therefore, weapons will not be blunted, and gains will be intact.
> These are the principles of planning attacks.
> — *Chapter: Attack by Stratagem* 《谋攻篇》

A person who is skilled in warfare would defeat the enemy without engaging in a fight or win the enemy's fortress without a prolonged battle. He would use a complete winning strategy. If he is able to do it, his soldiers would not be exhausted and opened to the enemy's assault. This is the principle of planning attacks.

To win 100 battles is not good enough. To win without direct engagement in a fight is considered the most dazzling.

The entrepreneur needs to realize that strategizing is a precursor to taking action. A consistent and brilliant strategy will directly impact the outcome of a competition. A good management strategy is not to have a direct engagement but to discover the competitors' weaknesses and locate breakthroughs in the market.

Hence, the entrepreneur, who is also the decision-maker, always takes unexpected action that surprises everyone. At times, the decision may seem unrelated to the daily operations but it is able to resolve difficulties and conflicts. The spark of brilliant idea normally comes from a thorough appreciation of market intelligence, an understanding of the competitors, and outstanding creativity.

Case Study 38: Taking The First Move. Advance When Others Retreat

In early 20th century, a young Chinese entrepreneur, Tan Kah Kee, was running a canned food factory in Singapore. He made good use of the available information and concluded that rubber plantations would be a lucrative business in Malaya.

With industrialization, the economic value of rubber has increased. Rubber has numerous uses in a newly industrialized world and the cost of owning a rubber plantation is low. The business is profitable.

Tan Kah Kee decidedly switched to rubber plantation business. Soon, the size of the rubber plantation increased to 5,000 acres.

The lucrative plantation business also attracted many Japanese and British investors. The number of rubber plantations began to grow and expand in Malaya. The large number of plantations also gave rise to a huge supply that stripped the demand. The price of rubber fell and Tan Kah Kee was loaded with excessive capacity. His rubber factory was suffering losses. Many owners in the business started to sell their plantations and factories.

The rubber plantation business is an important source of revenue for the British colonial government. It is unlikely that they will allow the price to keep falling. There is still a large market for other rubber products. I dare say that the current excess supply is temporary and will soon be a thing of the past.

Tan Kah Kee stood by his earlier decision to invest in rubber plantations.

Tan Kah Kee boldly bought another nine rubber factories and invested tens of thousands of dollars in upgrading and expanding his existing factories.

He found that the end products made from rubber were dominated by the British. His plantations only supplied raw materials to the British manufacturers. Tan Kah Kee raised another 100,000 dollars to build a factory producing rubber products. His business became an integrated producer of rubber products from raw material, processing to manufacturing.

In November of 1922, the British government resolvedly ncreased the price of rubber and revived the industry. Tan Kah Kee's business grew quickly with the revival.

Advance when others retreat. Staying focused and expanding the organization at the right time are proofs of right decisions. Take note that the correct decision is founded on credible business intelligence, accurate insight and judgment!

Case Study 39: Selling The Company For Greater Growth

Traditionally, hotel owners wanted to have ownership of land and hotel buildings. However, American hotelier, Marriot, had his unique conviction.

A company that continuously looks for investment and operating capital may increase the asset and value. This, however, may not be an advantageous strategy for the whole company.

For a listed company, the shareholders are not interested in appreciation of capital but the appreciation of the share prices. Hence, the operation efficiency is more important than simply asset appreciation for a company's development.

In the 1980s, following this conviction, Marriot sold most of his ownership in hotel property but retained the long-term rights of operation. This move freed up the company with billions of dollars to improve the hotels' facilities and management. The company now possesses less than 20 percent of physical hotel rooms but is cash rich to develop the business.

The common perception among entrepreneurs on expansion of the company's capability in business competition is through merger and acquisition. Marriot did the contrary. He divested his property and achieved success. To adopt this divestment strategy, the entrepreneur needs to know his company's core competencies and evaluate carefully the areas where the greatest value-add exists. Thereafter, adopt a flexible strategy to improve and reinforce these areas.

Case Study 40: Discover The Focus Of Management

Minou-Arima Railway was a new but small railway service provider in 1907. It was no way near its bigger city railroad counterparts operating in the populated town area. Hence, the company was operating in a difficult environment. Kobayashi Ichizou was the general manager.

> To put the business back on track, we have to increase revenue and profitability. There are two ways to achieve this: Increase the passenger load…

> Increase the train fare. This suggestion is not feasible for the sparsely populated area and would get backfired by the commuters. The question is how do we create more passengers.

Kobayashi shifted his focus from railroad to urban development of the area along the track. He changed the traditional way of residential property sales and embarked on a 10-year installment scheme to sell residential properties. His sales method encouraged ownership and he began to see more development around the area along the railroad. The increased occupancy for the residential projects led to increased passenger volume.

Kobayashi also built zoos and hot spring resorts along the scenic spots of the rail track.

Kobayashi further developed other community amenities like sports stadiums, recreational resorts and cultural centres. These facilities further boosted passenger volume.

The building of amusement parks, sports stadiums and residential homes all seemed unrelated to a railway operation. These projects, however, added more passengers and revenues to the railway business. The carefully designed strategy avoids vicious competition and simple price reduction. Instead, a serious tactic scores a homerun for the day.

The Art of Formulating Strategy
Section 3   Thorough analysis before setting target

> 夫未战而庙算胜者，得算多也；未战而庙算不胜者，得算少也。多算胜，少算不胜，而况于无算乎！吾以此观之，胜负见矣。
> Before doing battle, in the temple one calculates and will win, because many calculations were made;
> before doing battle, in the temple one calculates and will not win, because few calculations were made; many calculations, victory, few calculations, no victory, then how much less so when there are no calculations. By means of these, I can observe them, beholding victory or defeat!
> — *Chapter: Initial Assessment* 《始计篇》
>
> 故经之以五事，校之以计，而索其情……
> 凡此五者，将莫不闻，知之者胜，不知之者不胜。故校之以计，而索其情。
> Therefore, go through it by means of five factors;
> compare them by means of calculation, and determine their status
> All these five no general has not heard;
> one who knows them is victorious, one who does not know them is not victorious.
> Therefore, compare them by means of calculation, and determine their status.
> — *Chapter: Initial Assessment* 《始计篇》

One sees winning before a battle because there are sufficient conditions for success. One does not see winning before a battle because there are insufficient conditions for success. The one who makes a detailed calculation and works with advantageous conditions can win. One who miscalculates and has insufficient winning conditions will fight a losing battle. The worst is to have neither calculations nor conditions. We can get an indication of the winning party from the analysis.

For a battle, we make comparisons of the five factors and seven stratagems to understand the battle situation. The five factors and seven stratagems comprise: unity of soldiers, weather conditions, advantageous terrains, commanders and general capabilities, military discipline, fighting weapons and training quality. The generals and commanders must understand the five factors and seven stratagems to win. The factors and stratagems can help us understand the strengths and weaknesses and overall battle situation.

There are many common areas in business competition and war. We make similar analyses of strengths, weaknesses, opportunities and threats in the business environment for a better understanding of our business competitors and operating environment.
With a clearer understanding, we can adopt a winning strategy that employs the necessary initiatives to win the market.

Accuracy in judgment and calculation.

Case Study 41: A Clever But Seemingly Cowardly Action

Guang Zhou Shi Jin Cement Factory was a small enterprise. In 1984, its product won recognition as a "quality product". The employees were expecting that the factory manager, Lee, would expand the facilities and production. To everyone's surprise, Lee was careful and decided against any expansion plan at that moment.

The product won recognition as a "quality product". However, our level of quality is still inconsistent. Most of our workers used to be farmers and are lowly skilled. Expanding blindly with a weak workforce will not give sustainable growth. At this moment, we should put effort into training our workers for sustained quality.

For two subsequent years, the company's production volume remained unchanged. The company, instead, invested 300,000 dollars for its employees' skill upgrading. It invested a further 80,000 dollars to automate the factory and in production control. It was not until 1987 that the company built another processing line capable of 80 tons of production. The Chinese economy was over-heating in 1987. There was an explosion in the number of big infrastructure projects. This led to an increase in cement demand. Many customers wanted puzzolana cement as building material.

This type of cement was in high demand and cost 30 percent lower to produce compared to silicate-base cement. It all seemed advantageous to switch production but Lee rejected the idea.

The production methods for these two types of cement are different. It would be better for us to "clench our fist" and have mastery in one.

The prices of the building materials' began to decline and many building related companies were in financial difficulties. Shi Jin Cement Factory stood out among the competitors and had steady growth. Many companies came to Shi Jin to request for collaboration; some wanted to use the Shi Jin trademark while others were seeking techn(

If we accepted the requests, our engineers and I could receive huge financial rewards. However, our technology has yet to mature. A co-operation with immature technology will only mislead others.

Shi Jin Cement Factory's apparently conservative and cowardice responses in these three incidents gave the company more thrusts to improve internal processes and level of technology competency. The company achieved 100 percent passes in product quality assurance and was labeled a profitable company for eight consecutive years. Between 1989 and 1990, the company achieved recognition for being top in quality among more than 7,900 enterprises in heavy industry. When the rest of the players were experiencing bleak businesses, the company's product maintained its higher price and increased production by 10 percent each year.

When a "business opportunity" comes along the way, it is an entrepreneur's wisdom to carefully analyse the situation and in the process, devise a strategy that "improves the technology and quality".

Case Study 42: Preparation For Rainy Days

Chang Hong Electric of Si Chuan province was a major manufacturer of television sets in China. The management of the company had always been wary of changes and trends in the market.

Towards the end of 1988, the colour TV business which had been enjoying a boom, suddenly saw a drop in sales. Chang Hong was not spared the fate. The December sales volume was only 3 million dollars. The company analyzed and knew the cause.

The news that the government would soon levy purchase tax on colour televisions has made many TV distributors and sellers hesitant in purchase decisions. They are concerned that under the new tax law, they would need to bear extra taxes for new TVs.

Chang Hong Electric made an extensive study and analysis of the Chinese Colour TV market in the recent years. The study also included the production of TV sets.

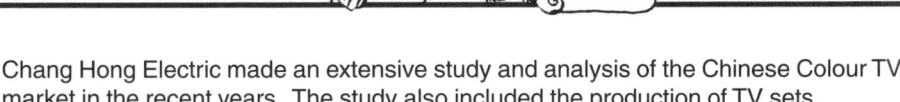

- Production for colour television sets
- Cost of production
- Product Models
- Functional Quality
- Marketing & Sales
- Demand & Quality
- Purchasing Power
- Purchasing Power

The conclusion was: The retail price of a colour TV would soon fall. Under this situation, if the company were to be the first to lower its price, this would help to boost sales. If the company were to wait for an industry-wide price drop, there would not be any advantage at all.

Chang Hong decided not to wait passively for things to happen. It made an announcement that the price of a colour TV set would be reduced by RMB 350. Chang Hong's 300-strong sales and marketing executives promoted their products in more than 20 provincial cities in China. The tight-pursed consumers were attracted by the lower price and sales soared. In 1988, the sales of Chang Hong reached RMB 840 million with a profit of RMB 147 million.

From the market study, Chang Hong recognized that a popular product in the market would eventually face its decline. Hence, it is important to revognize the "transition period" of a product change and make the necessary "move". Hence, while the company's 18-inch colour TV was still a hot seller, Chang Hong had already started to study the next market trend and make the appropriate investment in R&D.

In 1989, Chang Hong introduced the first remote-controlled stand-alone colour TV. The innovative design and easy-to-use functionality were well-received by consumers. While the old models of colour TV faced a glut in inventory, the new TV was hugely popular in many Chinese cities and was sold in more than 10 other countries. When the other TV manufacturers were still developing the stand-alone TV, Chang Hong Electrics had already begun its effort to develop the first flat panel TV in China.

One needs to be unyielding under the attacks from competitors. One also needs a strong defence to win others. A steadfast company analyses the market information and competitive trend. Developing new products is a two-prong strategy to defend and expand the market share.

Case Study 43: A Far-Sighted Management Decision

A new mining company was formed in the remote mountainous region in South Wales, Australia, more than a century ago. This company, BHP company, later became the mining giant in Australia. BHP had a long-term strategic objective and was able to follow through with the plan. The history in its business relationship with China clearly reflected its long-term objective.

BHP noted that China would develop into a huge market. As early as 1891, BHP had already exported iron ore to China. During the economic reform period in the 1980s, BHP built on its established trading relationship with China to expand its other business interests. BHP has good business relationships with two other Chinese companies, Shanghai Bao Shan Steel Company and Wu Han An Shan Steel Company. It was also involved in the construction of a large cement company and oil exploration venture in Bo Hai, off the coast of Tianjin.

In the second half of 1989, when many Western countries were exercising economic embargo on China, BHP firmly stood by its long-term strategy and maintained a cordial relationship with China. It went against the action of others in using economic means as a political leverage against China.

BHP maintained a positive outlook of its business in China. This confidence was founded upon a detailed analysis and judgment of the market. The analysis was a balanced and long-term one.

The company believed that China is an important member in Asia, which has a big market and huge economic potential. The decision to co-operate with the Chinese was an intelligent one. With this strategic belief, the company chairman, Sir Arvi Parbo, made numerous trips to China for business negotiations.

In business operation, the best strategy involves "multiple considerations". Is the product a necessity for the society?
Does the product suit the current age?
Are the manufacturing methods keeping pace with the current trend?
Are all levels of management equipped with the correct knowledge and experience?
Is the organization structure sound? Is the management direction correct?
With these judgments in hand, the entrepreneur is able to react calmly against unanticipated events.

The Art of Formulating Strategy

Section 4 Technology advancement is an edge for business competition

> 兵众孰强？士卒孰练？
> Which army is strong?
> Which officers and soldiers are trained?
> — *Chapter: Initial Assessment* 《始计篇》
>
> 故将通于九变之利者，知用兵矣；将不通九变之利，虽知地形，不能得地之利矣；治兵不知九变之术，虽知五利，不能得人之用矣。
> Therefore, the general who knows the advantages of the nine changes knows how to use the troops.
> If the general does not know the advantages of the nine changes, even if he knows the way of the land, he will not be able to take advantage of the ground.
> He who commands an army but does not know the principles of the nine changes, even if he is familiar with the five advantages, will not be able to best use his troops.
> — *Chapter: Nine Variations of Tactics* 《九变篇》

In the heat of the battle, the winner will be the army who has better training and better equipment. If the general understands the pros and cons of the nine terrains, he would know how to mobilize his army. He who does not know the way to use the nine changes will not have the advantage even if he understands the terrain. A commander will not be able to exercise the fighting power of his army without this knowledge.

In ancient warfare, both the opponents would have to seek initiative to gain the upper hand. Hence, there was strong emphasis on speed and fighting tactics. These factors were directly related to technology of the weaponry, a thorough understanding of weather and geography. When used in the business context, it could be explained as the emphasis and use of technology.

In business competition, technological edge is the key to sustained growth and initiative in actions. The quickened pace of technology advancement has transformed business competition into a race of technology. Whoever holds the key to technology leadership and develops the new products will have the upper hand in market competition.

Losing the leadership results in a passive position, one is destined to be left out of the market.

Emphasize on science and technology.

Case Study 44: The Father Of Japanese Motor Bike Industry

Honda Soichiro was the founder of Honda Corporation. He was widely known as "the father of Japanese motor bike industry". After he completed his apprenticeship with a car workshop, Honda set up a company known as Tokai Seiki. Honda sent 50 of his first batch of 30,000 pistons produced for testing at Toyota. Honda was told that only three out of the 50 samples passed the test.

The metal that produced the piston ring contained insufficient carbon and silica. This is basic knowledge and understanding.

If we install a small motor to the bicycle, it would be easier for the cyclist.

Japan, at that time, was in post war recession. To buy food and necessities, the people would have to travel long distances on a bicycle. Honda saw his future from the situation.

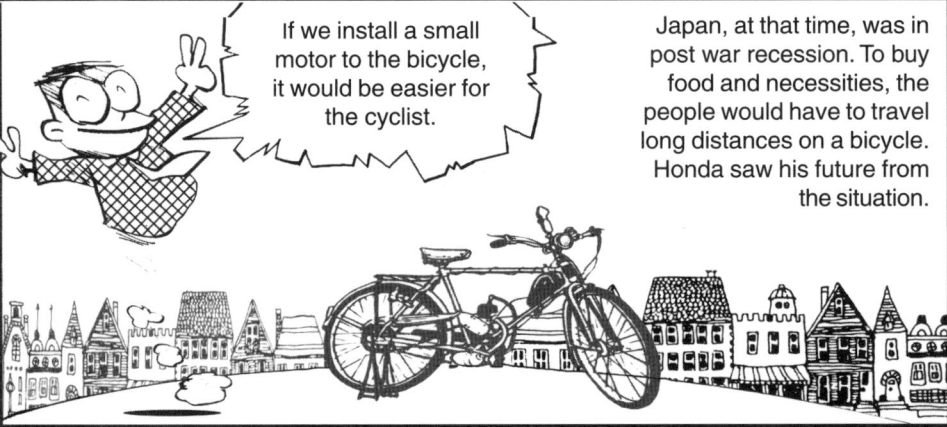

Starting from a simple motor for a bicycle, Honda introduced the undisputed motorcycle of the era in 1949. In 1951, Honda introduced the four-valves E model motorcycle. The quality of the product was ranked number one in Japan.

To get the product into the international market, he made visits to other motorcycle manufacturers in Britain and watched motorcycle races. He noticed that British bike makers had already developed 36-horsepower bikes while the best bike in Japan only had 13 horsepower. He was embarrassed by the technology of Japan. Honda was determined to develop the motor bike technology.

After five years of relentless effort, Honda racing bikes claimed the sixth position in the British Isle of Man Superbike Championship. Two years later, the Honda Race Team achieved astounding results by achieving the first to fifth positions in the 500CC, 125CC and 250CC categories. It went further to win the 125CC and 250CC World Grand Prix. Honda sales then had exceeded 100,000 motorcycles.

When everyone applauded the success of Honda Corporation, Honda recognized that danger loomed. He spent JPY 400 million to purchase new installations from America, Germany and Sweden to upgrade the old facilities in his bike plants.

Without the best production facility, we cannot produce the best product.

The purchase of expensive installations will be a big squeeze on the finances of the company. However, without these installations, the company will surely lose out in due time. There may be a danger of bankruptcy now; however, a proper management direction will lead us on a smoother route to success.

Advanced facilities and production technology are enablers for rapid improvements of product quality. These enablers help to expand the international market, transforming the company into the leader of its industry.

Case Study 45: The Battle Of Calculators

In September 1949, Tokyo organized its first product exposition. The four brothers of the Kashio family saw at the exhibition the expensive and bulky calculators produced by the Americans and Europeans. The brothers were determined to develop better calculators. After four ardent years of development work, they brought their prototype to show to some experts.

The brothers immediately embarked on their research and began to learn about the latest calculator technology. They further obtained financial support from a big Japanese trading company, Daiyo Shouji. In 1956, the Kashio brothers developed the solenoid calculator with continuous multiplication functionality. This latest calculator was put into commercial production.

The following year, "Casio 14-A" model, which featured 14-digit calculation and auto-off functions, was born. The Kashio brothers set up "Casio Calculator Holdings". By 1962, the company successfully introduced the "301" and "A-1" models. The company achieved annual sales of JPY 600 million.

In March 1964, Sharp Company successfully developed the world's first semiconductor transistor calculator that has a gross weight of 25 kg. The newest calculator Casio developed weighed 120 kg.

The Kashio brothers gave up the production of relay-type calculators in the face of changing customers' preference when Sharp introduced its new product. The brothers began their development effort in semiconductor transistor calculator, starting from ground zero again. In the technology race, all Casio employees began learning new electronics knowledge and battled many hurdles along the way. In October 1965, "Casio transistor calculator model 001" was born. The new model offered similar features as Sharp's product.

Let the calculator fit into everyone's pocket. Sharp had a new product slogan. The second generation of Sharp semiconductor calculators reduced the number of transistors from 4000 to only 59 integrated circuits cramped in 650 components. The weight was lightened to 4 kg and price reduced by 50%. This was the revolutionary moment in the history of calculators.

Casio was not to be left behind in the race. It stepped up its development effort with a technology tagline of "Develop a calculator that is handy for everyone and a housewife". In August 1972, the palm-size calculator which cost JPY 12,800 was introduced.

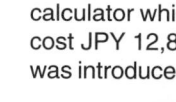

Sharp again raised the technology stake by setting its technology objective "to develop a thin calculator with liquid crystal display and uses dry cells". In 1975, Sharp introduced the all-new touch panel calculator. In May 1977, Sharp further introduced a calculator that was only 5mm thick and weighed only 60 grammes. This calculator had only three components. To fight back, Casio introduced the "name card" size, super thin calculator that was only 0.8 mm thick and weighed only 23 grammes.

When two companies with identical capital, talents and technology take on a common market, they created a "duo-poly". In this situation, the product and technology of both companies improve under mutual competition. This is a good example of a "win-win" situation.

Case Study 46: Exploring New Areas Of Technology

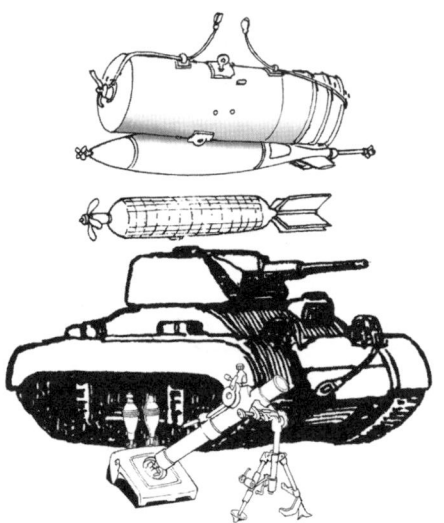

The year was 1820. Dupont developed a new explosive using their expertise in sodium nitrate and the glycerin-base explosive developed by Nobel. This new explosive had a different colour from the conventional black explosive. During the First World War, 50 percent of the explosives used by the Allied troops had been produced by Dupont. The company enjoyed huge profits with technology development.

Thereafter, Dupont Corporation explored other areas of technology innovation. It developed other products like composite fibres and pesticides. The composite materials developed in Dupont brought huge fortune for the company.

In its history of over 200 years since 1792, Dupont stood the test of time and difficulties. In 1986, the profit was USD 27.1 billion. Currently, Dupont is the leader in the chemical industry and ranks among the top 10 biggest producers of industrial products in America.

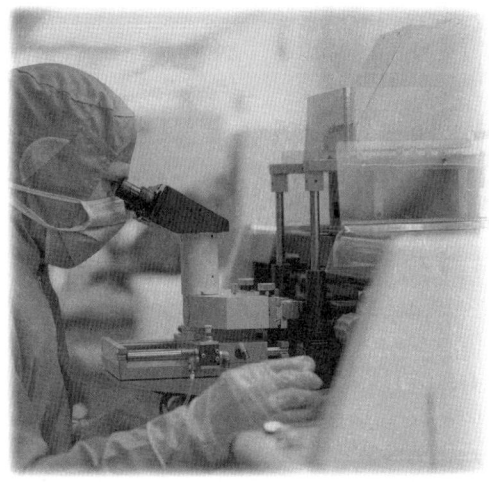

Dupont spends USD 1 billion on research and development yearly. There are more than 5,000 engineers working in research and development of new products and materials. The research laboratory is able to produce more than 1,000 types of composite materials per year, translating to two to three products per day. They could commercialize at least one product from the numerous innovations monthly.

After 200 years of development, Dupont has become the enterprise that produces and sells the largest number of products. Dupont products include: chemical fibres, medicines, petroleum products, car products, coal mining, industrial chemical products, paint, explosives and printing facilities. In recent years, Dupont has also moved into electronics industry. Excluding transportation and service sectors, Dupont has more than 1,800 products in the market.

Dupont has created an industry miracle and is a good case study for management. Its success is dependent on continuous research and development into new innovations and products. It develops what the market desires and is never complacent with successes of only one or two products.

Chapter 5
Competitive Strategy for Company

Section 1   Operating cost advantage

Section 2   Winning by surprise

Section 3   Strategy of partial competition

Competitive Strategy for Company
Section 1 Operation cost advantage

> 善用兵者，役不再籍，粮不三载，取用于国，因粮于敌，故军食可足也。
> Those skilled in doing battle do not raise troops twice, or transport provisions three times.
> Take equipment from home but take provisions from the enemy.
> Then the army will be sufficient in both equipment and provisions.
> — *Chapter: Waging War* 《作战篇》
>
> 故智将务食于敌。
> Therefore, a wise general will strive to feed off the enemy.
> — *Chapter: Waging War* 《作战篇》

A capable general organises his men and transports his war supplies only once. The fighting arms are transported from his own territory while the food supplies are obtained from the enemies' reserves. In such a case, there will not be problems in food supplies for the army. The intelligent general consumes the enemy's supplies and saves on his own logistics.

The above notion matches the objective of going to war. That is, to annihilate the enemy and expand one's own power base. This stratagem is known as the low consumption strategy in the Art of War. This strategy translated to business is operating cost advantage. To execute a successful business strategy and achieve a leadership position, you need to maintain an operating cost that is lower than your competitors'.

Case Study 47: Managing Expenses And Winning As A Small Player

Before 1933, China did not have its own chemical plant that produced oxygen and acetylene. The demand was met by the French-invested Orient Oxygen Company.

The demand for industrial oxygen grew steadily with many new factories being set up. Orient Oxygen's supply was not sufficient to satisfy the expanding market. Orient Oxygen raised the price and laid down harsh sales conditions for its products.

The consumers had no choice but to accept the harsh sales conditions of Orient Oxygen, which had a monopoly in Shanghai. At that time, there was a popular catchphrase among the industrialists.

"若要买气，就要受气"*

In 1933, businessman Xin Yun Chuang got his business associates together and started China Industrial Gas Holding.

To stave off its new competitor, Orient Oxygen started to lower the price of industrial oxygen.

One dollar and 30 cents per cubic metre.

80 cents per cubic metre.

*("气" qi has two meanings in Chinese; its original meaning "gas" and extended meaning "frustration". The phrase means "To buy gas is to court frustration.")

China Industrial Gas understood the importance of reducing the overall operating cost. The company achieved high productivity and low expenditures through the design of the gas plant and controlling daily expenses.

On the other hand, Orient Oxygen did not understand its opponent's strategy and neither did it realise the huge expenses and wastage inherent in its operation.

China Industrial Gas made an analysis of its cost structure and concluded that at a price of 80 cents per cubic metre, there would still be a small profit to be made.

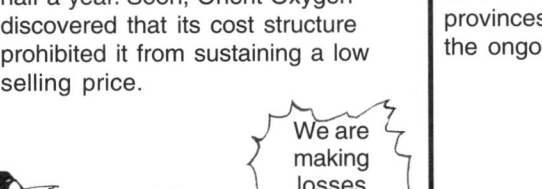

"What threat could China Industrial Gas Holding be?"

"Let's wage a price war!"

The price remained at 80 cents for half a year. Soon, Orient Oxygen discovered that its cost structure prohibited it from sustaining a low selling price.

On the contrary, China Industrial Gas was able to expand its market to the northern provinces of China (like Qing Dao), despite the ongoing price war.

"We are making losses again?!"

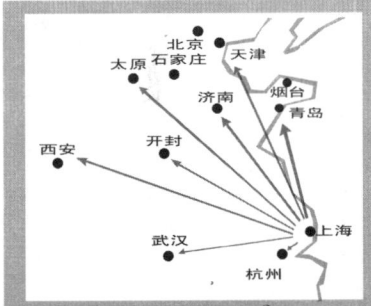

The keys for continual success in enterprise competition are lower costs, reduced expenses and improved productivity.

Case Study 48: Establishing A Steel Empire With Small Capital

American entrepreneur Andrew Carnegie painstakingly built his steel empire in the face of many obstacles. Ranked among the richest in America, he was always able to live up to challenges from competition.

We can take on the market anytime. We can win without competition.

This strategy of "win without competition" was based on Carnegie's low cost advantage. In the late 19th century, Carnegie concentrated his effort in restructuring his company and synergizing the production processes.

Carnegie made sure his suppliers from the coal and ore mines provided him with good quality raw materials and at a low price. He also unified and modernized the production processes used in blast furnaces and oxygen furnaces. Carnegie also transformed the discrete steps in steel making (which involves forging, rolling, cutting and casting) into a synergized process.

Carnegie implemented a cash flow analysis and kept a record of each processing step for the entire production. This helped him to understand the cost involved at each step and hence he was able to keep the cost at the lowest. He also believed in stressing the machinery and applying the right pressure on his employees to achieve maximum productivity.

Forging — Rolling — Cutting — Casting

A series of policies and changes helped to lower the production cost. In 1900, his production cost per ton of steel decreased from USD 56 to USD 11.50. The production output of his furnaces also increased from 13,000 tons to 100,000 tons. The customized production process and management system guaranteed an unparalled cost advantage.

Competitive Strategy for Company

Section 2   Winning by surprise

> 故善出奇者，无穷如天地，不竭如江河。终而复始，日月是也。死而复生，四时是也。声不过五，五声之变，不可胜听也；色不过五，五色之变，不可胜观也；味不过五，五味之变，不可胜尝也；战势不过奇正，奇正之变，不可胜穷也。奇正相生，如循环之无端，孰能穷之？
>
> Those skilled at uncommon manoeuvres are as endless as the heaven and earth, and as inexhaustible as the rivers and seas.
> Like the sun and the moon, they set and rise again.
> Like the four seasons, they pass and return again.
> There are no more than five musical notes, yet the variations in the five notes cannot all be heard.
> There are no more than five basic colours, yet the variations in the five colours cannot all be seen.
> There are no more than five basic flavours, yet the variations in the five flavours cannot all be tasted.
> In battle, there are no more than two types of attacks:
> Uncommon and common, yet the variations of the uncommon and common cannot all be comprehended.
> The uncommon and the common produce each other, like an endless circle.
> Who can comprehend them?
>
> — *Chapter: Use of Military Momentum* 《兵势篇》

A general who makes surprise winnings would have strategies that are ever-changing like the weather and flowing continuously like a river. They change momentously like the moving planets and overlap each other like how seasons change. There are five keys in musical notes but they can create an infinite arrangement of melodies. There are only five elementary colours but they could create infinite amalgamations of shades and lustre. The five types of tastes can also create infinite palates of savoury. In war strategies, there are only "qi" (奇) and "zheng" (正). "Qi" and "zheng" interact in a cyclical manner and form an endless relationship. What is there to disrupt this relationship?

Sunzi emphasized the element of surprise in an attack and trusted that this is the power to destroy the enemy and the secret to winning. For an entrepreneur, "qi" is the innovative management that encourages creativity and the improvement in new products that wins in competition. When the market requires a certain service or product, you are able to be the first to provide a product or service that meets the need of the market. You can find value and uniqueness in ideas that people discarded and thought to be useless. The action of "qi" is what others could not think, and the strategy of "qi" is what others cannot envisage.

"Winning by surprise" requires courage to be creative and to walk the unchartered territory. With the will to make new discoveries, then can the technology, management, operation and publicity of the company possess genuine vigour to "win by surprise".

The chain of "qi" and "zheng" evolves continuously.

Case Study 49: Revamp Of An Enterprise With Strict Code Of Conduct

In 1991, Nissan Company of Japan introduced FIGARO, a sedan car whose design was classical and gave an air of romance.

A unique news release was scheduled to usher a successful sales launch.

There will be only 20,000 FIGARO in the market! There will not be further production beyond this figure. We accept orders within a limited period only. With the overwhelming response, we will ballot for the buyers.

The news created huge interest and attention from consumers. The orders grew and exceeded 30,000.

The balloted buyers were extremely glad to be the lucky few. Those who were not lucky to be balloted hunted elsewhere for a resale car. The market price for a resale model rocketed to two times that of the original price. In that year alone, Nissan company sold more than 40 million cars and achieved sales revenue of JPY 427,000 million.

All men are equal in the eyes of the law. Similarly, all members in a company have to follow a strict code of conduct. When there is calmness within the organization, the company can face up to the pounding market forces.

Case Study 50: A Small Company Advertisement In Tiananmen

A huge culture and tour event was held in Bejing Tiananmen on 28 June 1994. The opening ceremony was scheduled at 9 am. The guests included many city and government officials.
An unprecedented scene was to be seen in the sky above the huge square.

Shuang Hui Pork Company was a small factory from Henan province. The abattoir's yearly sales was RMB 170 million and paid a tax of only RMB 4.63 million. The company heard of the cultural event in Tiananmen and sent its best marketer to negotiate with the event's organizing committee.

To add pomp to publicity, we are sponsoring 12 balloons, attached with our company's banners. We are also eager to sponsor RMB 10,000 for every balloon.

Many major newspapers and magazines reported on the flying balloons advertisement appearing in Tiananmen.

Tiananmen Square has been transformed into advertising panel!

This is the most successful and unique corporate publicity activity!

A first experience of advertising in Tiananmen Square!

Think what others have not, do what others have not. A company can enjoy many wonderful surprises with creative advertising strategies and good public relationships.

Case Study 51: Destroying Products In Large Volume

The beer market in China was booming in 1984. The Shang Dong Bo Xing Liquor Factory noted the trend and produced huge supplies of beer for the market. Unfortunately, the quality of the beer was not satisfactory. More than 180,000 bottles of beer were hoarded as inventory.

The unsold beer held up cash and space in the warehouse.

The liquor company came up with an idea to get rid of excess inventory.

Pour all the beer away!!

This action instilled in the employees the importance of "Quality Comes First".

Quality Comes First!

More importantly, it raised the social reputation of Bo Xing Liquor and created public interest and expectations of its new product. The liquor company successfully concocted a new recipe of quality liquor, known as "Yu Yie Jia Niang" and was well-received by the consumers.

In 1984, the company turned profitable. By 1987, the company paid taxes of 10 million yuan for its profit. The products can now be seen in all parts of China.

Competitive Strategy for Company

Section 3   Strategy of partial competition

> 非利不动，非得不用，非危不战。
> If it is not advantageous, do not move;
> if there is no gain, do not use troops;
> if there is no danger, do not do battle
> — Chapter: Attack with Fire 《火攻篇》
>
> 合于利而动，不合于利而止。
> If it is advantageous, move;
> if it is not advantageous, stop.
> — Chapter: Attack with Fire 《火攻篇》
>
> 所谓古之善用兵者，能使敌人前后不相及，众寡不相恃，贵贱不相救，上下不相收，卒离而不集，兵合而不齐。合于利而动，不合于利而止。
> In ancient times, those skilled in warfare were able to prevent the unity of the enemy's front and back troops, the many and the few, the noble and the peasants, and the superiors and the subordinates.
> Have the enemy separated and unable to assemble;
> if the enemy is assembled, it should not be organized.
> Move when advantageous, stop when not advantageous.
> — Chapter: Nine Types of Strategic Grounds 《九地篇》

If there were no advantageous situation, there would be no action. If there were no winnings, there would be no fighting. If there were no immediate crisis, there would be no engagement in a fight.

The ruler needs to take action if it is beneficial to the country and cease all actions when they do not benefit the country.

An experienced general can create disorder in the enemy's chain of command; the main force and sub-force in disarray, the officers and men in a state of confusion, the soldiers are smashed to smithereens and the formation in chaos. Even so for an experienced general, action should only be taken when there is a beneficial outcome.

"有利才行动，无利不妄动" (Take action when it is advantageous, hold position when it is disadvantageous). This is the only phrase in Sunzi's Art of War that has been repeated twice. This phrase also reflected the prudence of Sunzi's principle in waging a war. The application of this principle for business is to have limited competition for the company.

Competition is a means and not an objective for the survival and development of a company. Suitable and limited use of competitive advantage means leveraging on the strengths and weaknesses of the competitors. However, uncontrolled, anarchic and mindless competition is insane gamble.

Excessive competition destroys the company and causes wastage of the society's resources. Hence, there should be limited competition and avoid excessive conflicts. If there is no choice but to engage in a competition, one should judiciously choose a competitive environment and competitor.

Case Study 52: A Peaceful Pact And A Win-Win Situation

The founder of Indonesia's Lippo Group, Mochtar Riady (alias Li Wen Zheng), is a shrewd businessman who believes in fostering peace. Li maintained a cordial and successful relationship with Indonesians, Chinese and other foreign bankers and financiers.

> Fighting over profits with others would never make a lasting business case.

> To be in business means to take a long-term view. It also means to achieve a lasting advantage and not merely a one-off win.

> Business negotiation is not necessary a win-lose situation. It can also be a win-win situation.

His initial business was an import trading partnership with friends.

In 1960, Li and a few Chinese businessmen ventured into the banking industry. In 1971, Li gathered six of his business associates to form the Indonesian Finance Development (Pte) Ltd.

In the same year, Pan Indonesian Bank, Swiss-Fuji Bank together with a few other multinational banks jointly formed the Indonesian Finance Co-operation Private Limited. The purpose of the company was to look into investment projects in international capital financing.

In a short span of five years, Li successfully transformed Pan Indonesian Bank into the largest privately-held bank. Thereafter, Li Wen Zheng and Salim (alias Lin Shao Liang) partnered to form a finance and investment group. His assets then were well above USD 4 billion.

In business activity, competition comes naturally but is not all-powerful. When both competitors are equal in strength and capabilities, a sustained battle will lead to collapse for both parties.

Once both parties have reached an agreement, exercised their merits and worked together, it will be a win-win outcome.

Li's accordance to peace has maintained a balance between competition and co-operation. This gives a favourable result.

Case Study 53: Blind Competition Leads To Failure

Robert Campeau was one of the richest men in Canada. He was famous in property development. Campeau Corporation had been in the Canadian property development business for more than 40 years. By the 1970s, the company expanded and borrowed money from banks to purchase a piece of prime land in Manhatten, New York.

I have decided to raise USD 3 billion in capital to take over Federated Department Store Inc.

1986

In 1988, Robert Campeau continued with his expansion plan and engaged in a takeover bid with another department store chain, Macy, for control of Federated Department Store Inc. Finally, Campeau took over the company at a price of USD 6.5 billion and became the largest department store owner..

The expensive takeover was a big drain on Campeau's financial resources. The takeover brought financial difficulties for the company.

Let's borrow to make the payment!

Sell the company shares to raise more cash!

The takeover resulted in huge debt and liability for the company. By 1989, Campeau considered selling one of his two department stores to a Japanese retail conglomerate. The Japanese conglomerate capitalized on the situation and asked for a steep discount. Robert Campeau found the conditions unacceptable. Finally, he had to file for bankruptcy with the Federal Court.

Bankrupt

According to records, Robert Campeau owed a debt in excess of USD 10 billion. By selling the entire company and his personal assets, Campeau was still short of USD 1 billion. Robert Campeau moved into the unfamiliar retail business without due diligence and lost his entire property empire.

Case Study 54: Plunged Like A Diving Jet, Ignorance Is To Blame

In the 1970s, there were four major players in the Japanese motorcycle market namely Honda, Yamaha, Suzuki and Kawasaki. Among them, Honda was the largest maker and had 85 percent market share.

At the beginning of 1970, Honda decided to enter the saloon car market and invested in both technology development and production facilities. By 1975, the car market sales exceeded the motorcycle sales.

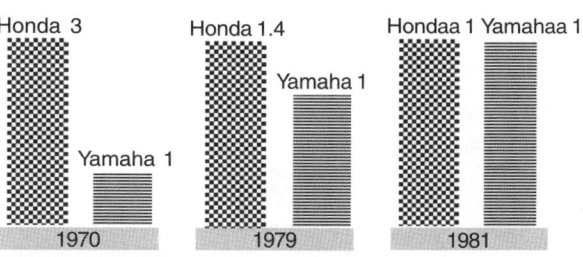

While Honda concentrated on developing the car market, it apparently neglected its leadership in the motorcycle market. The second-ranking Yamaha seized the opportunity to catch up with Honda.

Motorcycle salesa

	Honda	Yamaha
1970	3	—
1979	1.4	1
1981	1	1

"We cannot remain stagnant in the second place!"

In 1981, Yamaha invested in a motorcycle plant that had a capacity of 1 million motorcycles a year.

Honda had been the incumbent leader in the automobile business in Japan. It is also a financially strong company. Honda, with its superior technology in car making, made a punitive attack on Yamaha before its plant was due for completion. This was one of the deadliest corporate battles in Japanese corporate history.

Honda started a price war. At the peak of the competition, the selling price of a 50-litre Honda motorcycle was cheaper than a 10-gear bicycle. Besides its motorcycle business, Honda also had its car business to finance the price war in the motorcycle market. Yamaha, on the other hand, could only rely on motorcycle sales. Yamaha was at an obvious cost disadvantage.

Another strategy Honda adopted was to expand the product range and shorten the life cycle of each model. Within eight months, Honda rolled out 81 models of motorcycles while Yamaha trailed behind with only 34 models. The cost disadvantage, coupled with the dreary design, caused a down spiral of sales like a plunging jet. By the end of 1982, Yamaha incurred a debt of JPY 220 billion. The bank stopped the financing and the unsold inventory was piling.

In 1983, the chairman of Yamaha, Kawakame, bowed and made his apology to the chairman of Honda, Kawashima Kiyoshi, for Yamaha's inept action. The president of Yamaha, Koike was removed in June 1983. This battle that lasted for 18 months ended with Yamaha as the loser.

Prudence is a virtue for an entrepreneur in competition. A rational competition is one that is based on a fundamental understanding of the opponent. A blind and insane competition will manifest as agonizing consequences for the company.

Case Study 55 : A Deceptive Publicity Stunt Cannot Last Long

STP produced mainly additives for petrol and diesel. Between 1963 and 1970, under the leadership of Andy Granatelli, the sales increased from USD 9 million to USD 85 million. The profitability was USD 12 million in 1970. Granatelli had a very aggressive advertising campaign to boost the sales.

The STP advertising campaign comprised voice commercials on three major radio networks, TV commercials on two major TV networks and print advertisements in more than 30 car-racing magazines. In 1969, the advertising expenditure grew so much that the marketing cost of a can of STP additive was USD 0.18 more than its production cost. It could be said that the success of the product was largely due to the generous advertising effort.

"STP additives cannot improve the performance of the engine. It may in fact, damage car engines!"

In 1971, an article in "Consumer's Report" sounded its whistle against STP.

STP is effective when used with other petrol products. The number one choice for your car!

STP is a WONDER for car racers.

The problems with car engines that arise from STP additives would void the car warranty. General Motors and Ford Company made the warranty void declarations against STP additives.

In 1973, the Federal Trade Commission declared that STP misled the public with its advertising campaign. The sales of STP plummeted immediately.

In 1973, the flamboyant marketing wizard of STP, Andy Granatelli, left the company. The sales triumph of STP became history.

Shares of STP
1971 — USD 60
1973 — USD 3

Shares of STP
1971 — USD 11.6 million
1973 — USD 1 million

Chapter 6
Competitive Strategy in Business

Section 1 Enterprising attack and active defence

Section 2 Insist on quality and dare to innovate

Section 3 Strategy in price psychology

Section 4 Attack on weaknesses. Explore new markets

Competitive Strategy in Business

Section 1   Enterprising attack and active defence

> 昔之善战者，先为不可胜，以待敌之可胜。不可胜在己，可胜在敌。故善战者，能为不可胜，不能使敌之可胜。故曰：胜可知，而不可为。不可胜者，守也；可胜者，攻也。守则不足，攻则有余。善守者藏于九地之下，善攻者动于九天之上，故能自保而全胜也。
>
> In ancient times, those skilled in warfare make themselves invincible and then wait for the enemy to become vulnerable.
> Being invincible depends on oneself, but the enemy becoming vulnerable depends on himself.
> Therefore, those skilled in warfare can make themselves invincible, but cannot necessarily cause the enemy to be vulnerable.
> Therefore it is said one may know how to win but cannot necessarily do it.
> One takes on invincibility defending, one takes on vulnerability attacking.
> One takes on sufficiency defending, one takes on deficiency attacking.
> Those skilled in defence conceal themselves in the lowest depths of the earth.
> Those skilled in attack move in the highest reaches of the heavens.
> Therefore, they are able to protect themselves and achieve complete victory.
> — *Chapter: Disposition of Military Forces* 《军形篇》
>
> 故善攻者，敌不知其所守；善守者，敌不知其所攻。
> Therefore, against those skilled in attack, the enemy does not know where to defend; against those skilled in defence, the enemy does not know where to attack.
> — *Chapter: Weaknesses and Strengths* 《虚实篇》

An expert at war would not allow the opponent a winning chance. Instead, he will wait for the right moment to make a winning strike. The controlling stake of allowing the enemy to strike is on oneself. To win the enemy is to capitalize on his mistake. A person who knows what to do in a battle would ensure that he is not defeated though he does not necessarily become the absolute winner. Hence, it can be said that winning is foreseeable but not an absolute must. If one is sure that he is unable to defeat the enemy, he has to build up his defence. If one is sure that he is able to defeat the enemy, he has to launch his attack. With the same number of troops, it might be sufficient in defence but insufficient in attack. An experienced warrior would conceal his troops with the nine strategic grounds. When he launches his attack, the troops would emerge from obscurity. He will initiate an attack on his unknowing enemy. When he actively builds up his defence, the enemy would not know how to attack his stronghold. Hence, an intelligent person is able to protect himself and win an absolute victory.

    Be it a real battle or in a business competition, we can have either an attack or a defence scenario. The entrepreneur needs to assess his position relative to his opponent in the competitive environment. After a detailed study of the factors influencing the battle, he can then devise the attack or defence strategy correctly. In a business competition, it does not necessarily mean that defence is only applicable in a disadvantaged position. When one is the market leader, he must also be making his defensive preparation. This is known as active defence.
If the company has the capability to challenge but is not in the market leadership position, it should make his attack. This is known as active attack strategy.

> The one who is well versed in attack and defence wins.

Case Study 56: A Lightning-Like Attack

In December 1988, a German cargo vessel sailed from America to Tian Jin Port. Upon unloading the cargo, the owner of the vessel wanted to sell the vessel away. The vessel owner signed a memorandum of understanding with a potential buyer from India.

The president of China's Yue Da Company, Hu You Lin got information of the sell-off and instinctively knew that it was a bargain buy. Without hesitation, he sent a faxed intent of purchase to the vessel owner and explained the benefits of selling the vessel in the port immediately after unloading the cargo.

Hu made his courtesy call on the owner at the cargo vessel in Tian Jin port. After a long negotiation, he managed to convince the owner to sell the vessel at a price that was USD 200,000 lower than the offer price of the prospective Indian buyer.

I am glad that the deal is successfully sealed!

This cargo vessel was later christened by the renowned Chinese General Zhang Ai Ping as "Yan Fu".

Yue Da Group is indeed incredible!

In March 1992, the German lingerie manufacturer, Triumph International, wanted to partner a Chinese company to produce 10 million pieces of Triumph undergarments. The investment was said to be USD 8 million. Guenther Spiesshofer, president of Triumph International, came to Shanghai.

Hu was on a train from Beijing to Tai Hu. He recognized that an opportunity was knocking on the door and made his trip to Shanghai via Beijing. The whole journey took less than five hours and he was already anxiously waiting for Mr Spiesshofer at his hotel. An agreement was inked on the 10 March 1993 where both parties agreed to set up a company that manufactures ladies' garment in China. This company is called "Yan Cheng International Ladies Wear Limited".

Earlier in 1992, Yue Da Company had also secured a joint venture with an Indonesian car manufacturer. Hu, upon securing the approval by the government, led his team to Indonesia and discussed the joint venture with their Indonesian counterpart. The joint venture began the production of vans and soon established a sizeable production facility.

A successful company scores a streak of winnings by consistently capturing the opportunities. When the company is accurate in forecasting the market trend and understands its strengths and competitive advantages, it is able to take the initiative and develop rapidly.

Case Study 57 : Guarding The Technology Secrets

Michelin Tyres in France has a history of more than 180 years. In 1980, its sales ranked first among tyre makers in the European community and second in the world after its American rival, Goodyear.

To ensure product leadership, Michelin invested large capital to build a research laboratory that was equipped with advanced facilities. Besides the laboratory equipment, it has a test track and a team of test drivers.

The integrated test centre was manned by more than 600 test drivers and 30 engineers. It is also a facility that has a 32- kilometre test track catered to more than 700 different in-house car models. The test track can be used to collect data for different driving conditions for the tyres. These conditions include initial startup, cruising, braking, turning, acceleration and driving on slippery road.

Michelin had more than 10,000 employees involved in research and engineering. This figure was about 10 percent of its worldwide employees. Research spending was 5 percent of gross sales.

The advanced and innovative R&D effort gave the company its dynamic competitive edge. The radial tyre was an innovation by Michelin. The radial design gave Michelin tyres a lifespan that was two times longer than conventional tyres. At the 1975 World Expo in Paris, the 5-metre diameter radial tyre was reputed as the "king of tyres".

Michelin guards its technology secret supremely. The research centre rejects tours by foreign visitors. Within the company, there is no overlap of processes to ensure no technology information leakage.

Top Technology Secret! No information leakage!

In 1964, then French President, DeGaulle, was making his official visit to central France. To give publicity to Michelin, he had wanted make a study tour of Michelin's facilities. To everyone's surprise, his request for a visit was regretfully but courteously turned down by the company.

If you were making your visit alone, it would be our best honour. However, we believe that you would be accompanied by an entourage of officials and members. It would be difficult for us if one of the visitors harbours any intention to steal information from here.

The highly guarded technology secret was Michelin's defence against competition.

Case Study 58 : Multiple Defence Lines To Reduce Risk

Shell Company is the largest energy company in the world. In 1990, its total revenue was USD 107 billion and was second only to General Motors. As a multinational oil company, it is constantly subject to risks. Shell Company set up three lines of defence against these risks.

The first line of defence. The management headquarters are spread all over the world. Shell Company has oil exploratory and drilling operations in more than 50 countries. It has oil refineries in 34 countries and the products are sold in more than 100 countries. The decentralized production and sales locations mitigated risks in the event of any political chaos or economic upheaval in a particular geographical region.

The second line of defence. The company has a wide range of products and services. Besides its core business in oil refinery, it also has businesses in coal, chemical and metal industries. This decreases the risk associated with a single product line.

The third line of defence. The company set up a quick response system in case of emergency. Shell Company observes the regional political and economic event unfolding closely and analyzes the impact these events would have on its operations. Every year, the company would carry out four "crisis exercises" and trigger its "emergency response plans" to check its state of readiness. These "exercises" help its fleet of 122 oil tankers improve their response time in case of emergency.

The commonality of knowing how to run a business and experience in running a business is: proactive in defence and developing the company's strengths. Shell Company's three lines of defences are its absorbers that withstand the shocks from political tremors and helped the company move forward to greater development. These further improve the company's competitive edge and capability.

Competitive Strategy in Business

Section 2 Insist on quality and dare to innovate

> 三军之众，可使必受敌而无败者，奇正是也
> What enables an army to withstand the enemy's attack and not be defeated are uncommon and common manoeuvres.
> — *Chapter: Use of Military Momentum* 《兵势篇》
>
> 凡战者，以正合，以奇胜
> Generally, in battle, use the common to engage the enemy and the uncommon to gain victory.
> — *Chapter: Use of Military Momentum* 《兵势篇》

When the soldiers are attacked by the enemy and remain undefeated, this is the outcome of appropriate "surprise-predictability" (奇正 qi-zheng) strategy. We engage the enemy with "predictability" and win the enemy by "surprise".

There are multiple meanings to "predictability"(正) and "surprise" (奇) described in the Art of War. From the strategic perspective, an open declaration of war is "predictability"; a sudden attack is "surprise". When used to describe the strength of troops, the main force is "predictability"; and the supporting force is "surprise". When used to discuss warfare, conventional warfare is "predictability"; unconventional warfare is "surprise".

Maintaining quality is the basis for competition in business. It is considered as conventional management stratagem. A high standard of quality for products and services must be maintained for sustained market share. On the other hand, to enter into a new market and introduce a new product, there is need for more innovation and creativity. This is the "surprise" element in an unconventional management stratagem.

Case Study 59: Maintain Quality And Be Bold To Explore

The American computer manufacturer DEC was established in 1957. The sales at the beginning was only USD 70,000. It was another typical American company then. Computers were big and expensive then. The use of a computer was once a sophisticated skill and required much technical knowledge.

The founder of DEC, Olsen, decided to put his focus into developing affordable microcomputers for small enterprises. In 1960, DEC successfully developed PDP — model 1. By 1965, DEC successfully developed PDP — model 8. DEC then started to develop other computer systems with capabilities that suit the preferences of different computer users.

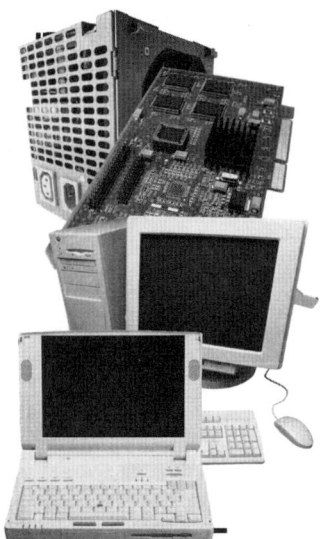

It was uncommon for manufacturers to develop products that catered to the minority among consumers. To everyone's surprise, DEC grew at a stunning rate and captured a market share of close to 40%. The product range offered by DEC was wide; the cheapest computers were selling at only USD 400. The most expensive product was sold at USD 1.5 million. The quality and reliability of DEC computers were excellent. PDP — model 8 was well-liked by consumers. By 1980, DEC sales surpassed USD 2 billion.

A strategist that adopts "the common to engage the enemy and the uncommon to gain victory" will untiringly develop and introduce new products. Concurrently, the quality of existing products is maintained.

Case Study 60: Quality Is The Lifeline Of A Company

Kuroda Precision Company was the largest manufacturer of basic measuring devices. Over the years, besides maintaining its leadership in making simple measuring devices, Kuroda also developed into a high accuracy metrology equipment maker with worldwide presence.

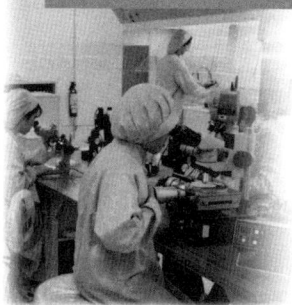

Kuroda Precision made technology leadership its core competency. The company developed cutting edge technology on its own or worked with partners to bring in new technology. It brought in the latest facilities and metrology tools from Germany.

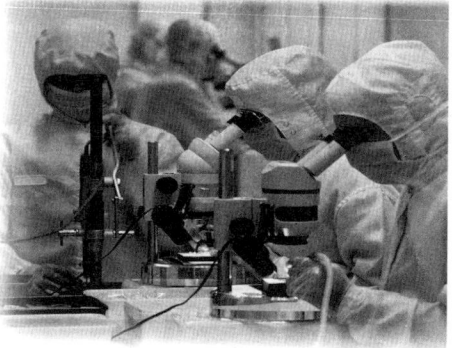

Kuroda Precision invested in an expensive production area where the temperature and humidity are carefully controlled. To ensure good quality, it raised the tolerance of the parts produced to less than 0.004 mm. Production operators, quality inspectors and technologists must follow strictly to the specification. Kuroda Precision used advanced computer systems to control its production planning, and advanced assembly equipment to produce products that were of the highest level of technology.

In **Kuroda Precision**, there is this maxim: "Quality is the lifeline. Technology is warranty". The company was successful in realizing the statement. In this way, it firmly controlled the local market and speedily penetrated into the international market. This is a union of "diligent in defence and initiative in attack" in management strategy.

Case Study 61: "Super Knowledge" Management Style

In 1981, Roberto Goizueta became the chairman of Coca Cola Company at the age of 84. Before taking on the position, Goizueta was a technical manager with little management experience. The entire industry and watchful media were waiting to see how this technical manager was going to fumble in managing the world's largest soft drink company. Once he took up the role of chairman, Roberto Goizueta announced a series of creative management strategies.

Our strategies

While others adopted a wait-and-see attitude, Coca Cola took the lead and became the first to penetrate the huge market of 10 billion-population in China.

We are in the soft drink business. Why are we buying a movie company?

There are many common grounds between selling movies and selling drinks. In both cases, we operate by lowering cost and developing new markets. We will turn all movie patrons of Columbia Pictures into Coca Cola drinkers.

Coca Cola invested large capital in taking over one of the three big names in Hollywood's film industry — Columbia Pictures.

The Coca Cola head office began to get involved with the distributors' operations when necessary.

"For decades, Coca Cola has not interfered with the distributors' operations."

"For distributors who are not active in promoting our Colas, we will have to let them go."

When the Philippines distributor's sales dropped from 46% to 33%, the distributorship was terminated.

The head office set up a new office in the Philippines. Within six months, the sales improved.

"We will set up a new distribution office to take over the operation there!!"

Knowledge in management is a requisite for all entrepreneurs but this knowledge is not stagnant. To continually drive the company, the entrepreneur needs to build upon the existing knowledge and add on new meanings. This notion is known as "super knowledge". This is expressed as "predictability in engagement, surprises in victory" in "Art of War".

Competitive Strategy in Business

Section 3   Strategy in price psychology

> 故三军可夺气，将军可夺心
> The energy of the army can be dampened, and the general's mind can be weakened.
> — *Chapter: Manoeuvreing* 《军争篇》

We can influence the morale of the enemy's troop and affect the general's determination. "Matters of heart" refers to thinking, determination, morals, sentiments and all other psychologies of a person. These matters of heart are what determine the actions and decisions of a general, which ultimately influence the outcome in the battle. Hence, we can achieve victory by disturbing the psychology of the general.

In price psychology, "sell cheap and generate volume" is an essential and common tactic adopted by many companies. The essence of this tactic is: drive up sales by having a lower profit initially and to grow the business thereafter. In management strategy, we term it as taking a long-term view. In adopting this price strategy, the seller will set a cheap but reasonable price. This is followed by good after-sales services to win the consumers' goodwill. Once the consumers are acceptable to the product psychologically, a long lasting seller-buyer relationship is possible. In essence, the purpose of using price psychology is to establish stable long-term growth and result.

Case Study 62: Low Price High Volume Strategy

The sales of electrical goods were sluggish in the 1950s because these products were considered expensive for many families. The general manager of Daiichi Sangyo Company of Japan, Kubo Michimasa, believed in the "low price-high volume" strategy. He managed to expand the market share quickly and achieve profitability.

Kubo's strategy invited many criticisms from other people in the industry. He was also taken to court many times by some of his competitors.

"Ask the home appliance manufacturers to cut supply to Daiichi Sangyo!"

"I am only selling at a slightly lower price than the market and providing customer satisfaction to consumers. We are where we are only because the customers are satisfied."

Kubo was firm in his belief. The court finally ruled that to stop order for the suppliers to Daiichi Sangyo was a violation to the "Anti-monopoly Act". Kubo won his case against his plaintiffs. Kubo's strategy worked and sales increased more than 25 times of the fixed capital.

"The court's ruling: Daiichi Sangyo Company has won the case."

Daiichi Sangyo continued with its price strategy. Besides that, the company spared no effort in providing after-sales services in spare parts distribution and maintenance business.

In the 1960s, Kubo was the first to come up with "Door-to-door Maintenance Services". He further established the call-on-demand repair services that gave year-round home repair services.

This revolutionary service was lauded by consumers and in turn brought good name to the company. The sales continued to climb steadily.

A price war not only brings success for the company. More importantly, it brings long-term goodwill to the customers and branding for the company. A price war is also a psychology war!

Case Study 63: Sales Promotion For Luxury Products

A jewellery dealer from the Arizona State in America purchased a batch of top grade turquoise stones. The purchased quantity was large and the owner was worried that the unsold stones would hold up the cash in the short run. The owner decided to lower the price to generate sales.

However, things did not turn out as he expected. A few days passed but the buying fever was not visible with the lower price. The owner was confounded.

Could the lower price be still too expensive to attract buyers?

Don't forget!!

An urgent overseas business deal needed the attention of the owner. While rushing off to discuss the business deal, the owner had no time to tell his staff what to do. He simply left them a note.

Sell turquoise stones 1/2 times

Once, twice. The sales staff raised the price two times. Buyers formed a beeline outside the shop. The sales staff raised the price again. In a matter of days, the turquoise stones were all sold out. The owner came back from his business trip and a pleasant surprise was waiting for him.

Not one to two times but half the price!!

A company that specialized in marinated food in China exported its products to the Australian market. The seasoned vegetables were not only tasty but inexpensive too. However, the sales were disappointing.

A price reduction did not help the situation but scared away more customers.

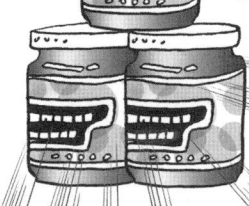

Before, housewives in Australia were buying these products as gifts for friends and relatives. A cheaper price and simpler packaging made the product less attractive as a gift.

The company's marketing people began to raise the price and repackage the product. These changes helped to push up the sales.

The Chinese company conducted a market study and realized what the local preference was. This shed some light on the cause of the lower sales.

An entrepreneur needs to study the market psychology. Price is not the single factor that affects sales. It works with other factors like market preference and consumers' behaviour. The price needs to be analyzed technically, taking into account consumers' psychology.

Case Study 64: Tactics In Rounding The Price Figure

In a summer season, a retailer purchased a batch of mattresses to be sold for the hot weather. The selling price of a mattress was USD 1. The demand of mattresses is seasonal and they sell well in summer. However, that year, the buyers were not interested.

We need to lower the price to improve sales.

At the present cost price, the best we can do is to lower the price by two cents.

By lowering the price, the mattresses were quickly snapped up.

Amazing, what a difference two cents can make.

We discovered that a product will sell better at 49 cents, than at 50 cents. For products that are sold at five dollars or lower, prices with cent-digit ending with "9" will drive consumers' impulse to buy. For products that are sold at five dollars or more, prices with cent-digits ending with "95" give better appeal to buyers.

Studies conducted by American business psychologists concluded:

Prices with cents difference rounded to a full dollar is considered as a seller's price. Since the price is set by the seller, a full-dollar price will not appeal to the buyer.

The Japanese business psychologists also concluded:

Price with cent-digits starting with "0" is considered the buyer's price and can drive the purchase impulse. We call this pricing scheme as "unrounded pricing method".

The price may be close to a full dollar but it gives different psychological messages to consumers. For example, a price set at $0.98 gives the impression that the product costs less than $1. However, if the price is set at $1.01, it gives the impression message that the product costs more than $1.

Furthermore, an unrounded price signifies to a buyer that the seller is prudent and careful in deciding his selling price. The sincerity in setting a price helps to establish faith between the seller and buyer.

The "unrounded pricing method" tells a buyer that the price is fair. These consumers' psychology findings give the entrepreneur not just a method in setting prices but also deeper thoughts into consumer behaviour and sales strategy.

Competitive Strategy in Business

Section 4   Attack on weaknesses. Explore new markets

> 进而不可御者，冲其虚也；退而不可追者，速而不可及也。
> To achieve an advance that cannot be hampered, rush to the enemy's weak points.
> To achieve a withdrawal that cannot be pursued, depart with superior speed.
> — *Chapter: Weaknesses and Strengths* 《虚实篇》
>
> 知战之地，知战之日，则可千里而会战；不知战之地，不知战日，则左不能救右，右不能救左，前不能救后，后不能救前，而况远者数十里，近者数里乎！
> if one knows the place of battle and the day of battle, he can march 1,000 li and do battle.
> If one does not know the place of battle and the day of battle, then his left troops cannot aid his right, and his right troops cannot aid his left;
> his front cannot aid his back, and his back cannot aid his front.
> How much less so if he is separated by tens of li, or even a few li.
> — *Chapter: Weaknesses and Strengths* 《虚实篇》

Advance when the enemy is defenceless as this is the area where the enemy is the weakest. Retreat when the enemy is unable to pursue as this is the area where the enemy is not on their guard.

It is not a problem to engage the enemy, even if it needs to travel thousands of "li" when we know the precise time and area to attack. On the contrary, we would not be able to advance even a few "li" as we will be too busy to defend our weaknesses.

In competition, we avoid the competitive environment where the market is saturated or the competitors are strong. We move into a new market or where the competitors are weak. Avoid the strong but attack the vulnerable positions of the competitor. Turn strengths to weaknesses and weaknesses to strengths.

An entrepreneur needs to cast his vision far and wide, moving beyond the local market and into a wider market. Set the vision on the world market and compete globally. As long as we understand the international market and its requirements, we can still win in that competitive environment.

Case Study 65: Avoid A Strong Competitor, Look For Alternatives

In October 1849, the government of Prussia (in what is now parts of southern Lithuania) officially allowed the use of telegraph line in Aachen (the area between Berlin in Germany and Brussels in Belgium). The paid telegraph line could also be used for commercial purposes. The new telegraph line gave importance to the Aachen region and transformed telecommunication services between Berlin and Aachen into a lucrative business.

Paul Julius Reuter heard this news and recognized that it was a great business opportunity. He decided to work on this opportunity and went to Berlin. He had wanted to set up a news agency in Berlin.

However, the owner of "Wolf News Agency", Mr Wolf, had made the move before Reuter.

Reuter realized that he had no means to compete with Wolf. Reuter did not give up. Instead, he decided to go to Aachen.

Wolf is a smart man and has a rich family behind him.

As Reuter anticipated, no one had set up a news agency in Aachen. He immediately started a small independent news agency.

Reuter utilized the most efficient telecommunication means available to consolidate business news and intelligence from European cities. The information was then compiled into quick quotes and news that were sent to subscribers.

Reuter worked very hard and soon his business in news services took shape. As time passed, the demand for his news summaries and quotes grew. He finally set a firm footing in the news and information business.

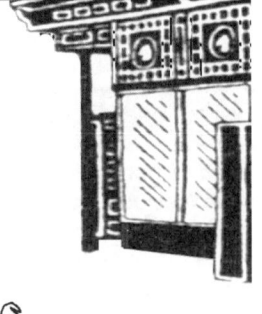

I was faced with a formidable opponent and had no means to win in the competition. At that time, I needed to exercise discretion and nimbly find an alternative to avoid direct competition.

To explore a new market where the competition is limited makes my dream easier to realize.

Case Study 66: A Peasant Woman Who Became The "Goddess Of Fortune"

Yang Gui Yu was commonly known as Aunty Yang. She came from Gao Zhou prefecture in Guang Dong province. In 1989, she had a bumper harvest of tomatoes and bananas at her hometown. There were so much vegetables and fruits that could not be sold completely in Guang Dong.

We cannot leave these fruits and vegetables to rot.

Aunty Yang knew that there was demand for tomatoes and bananas in Beijing. She made her way to Beijing with her tomatoes and bananas, despite objections from her family.

I'm going to make my fortune in Beijing!

With a peasant background, Yang had no business experience. She lost half a truck load of bananas when she arrived in Beijing. The loss cost her RMB 10,000. She was not disheartened and borrowed RMB 100,000 from the bank to start her fruit distribution business in Beijing.

Yang made excellent use of accurate market intelligence and sent her fresh fruits and vegetables at a low cost to customers. She also provided good services to the buyers in Beijing. Yang went a step further to link up a telephone line in her mountainous village. The better communication means paid off. She was able to supply her fruits and vegetables timely to Beijing within four days when the demand is high. Yang was able to sell more than 2,000 tons of fruits and vegetables in the Chinese capital within a year.

Accurately target the markets and hit out on the weaknesses to deliver good quality but price effective goods and services. With the effort, one takes the initiative, seize the market and win a victory.

Case Study 67: Cast Your Vision In International Market

Holland is a small country in Europe with a low ground. It is, however, the home country of world-renowned electrical appliance maker, Philips Electronics.

How did Philips emerge from a homegrown company in a small country to become a global brand? The company's chairman correctly summarized the reason:

The fact that Holland is a small country makes it necessary for us to look beyond our local market and into the international markets.

In the 1920s, Philips had only sales offices in other countries. The manufacturing plants were all in Holland.

In the 1930s, trade restrictions were common following the Great Depression. To overcome the controls and regulations, Philips started to invest in manufacturing plants overseas.

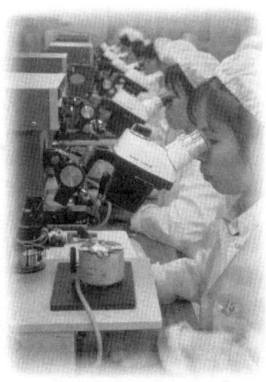

In the 1950s, Philips took the opportunity arising with the formation of European Community (EC) to set up a one-stop R&D, manufacturing and sales facility in the member countries. Henceforth, the overseas expansion strategy in Philips took shape. It developed into a global company that saw no boundary.

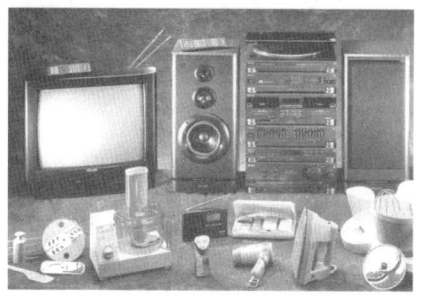

In the 1960s, Philips acquired and merged other businesses into its stable of companies. These businesses included Chappell Recording Company and Australian Electronics & Industrial Company. These acquisitions enhanced Philips' capabilities.

In the 1980s, Philips set its eye on the stronghold of the Japanese makers, specifically, the consumer appliances market. The appreciating Yen then resulted in a decrease in exports for the Japanese appliances. Philips started its penetration into this lucrative market. The first market it captured was the South East Asian market. It slowly made progress into even the Japanese market. In its expansion, Philips continued to lead in technology and created many breakthroughs in new product development.

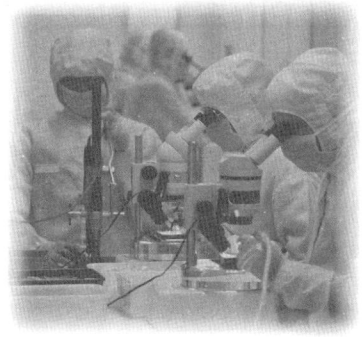

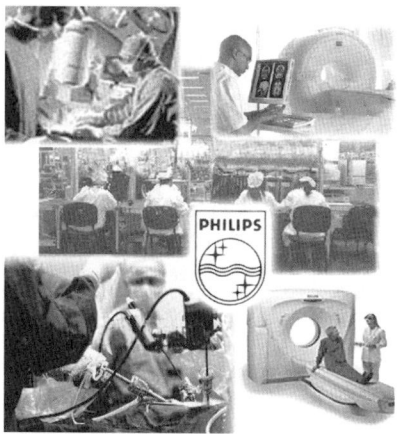

In its corporate history of more than 100 years, Philips had transformed from a manufacturer of batteries into an established manufacturing giant for different products. To name a few, Philips sells audio products, home electrical appliances, industrial electronics, chemical and pharmaceutical products. In 1991, the company's sales exceeded USD 30.8 billion and it was ranked 28th among famous industrial companies.

Philips recognized that the small market in Holland was limited and set its long-term objective to develop the international market. Philips sensibly selected its strategy and became a victorious warrior in exploring and developing a global market.

Chapter 7
Market and Information Analysis

Section 1   Adjust product and services to changes

Section 2   Analyze the environment and know your competitors

Section 3   Analyze the overall market scientifically and accurately

Market and Information Analysis

Section 1 Adjust product and services to changes

> 故明君贤将所以动而胜人，成功出于众者，先知也。先知者，不可取于鬼神，不可象于事，不可验于度，必取于人，知敌之情者也。
> What enables the enlightened rulers and good generals to conquer the enemy at every move and achieve extraordinary success is foreknowledge.
> Foreknowledge cannot be obtained from ghosts and spirits;
> it cannot be inferred from comparison of previous events, or from the calculations of the heavens, but must be obtained from people who have knowledge of the enemy's situation.
> — *Chapter: Use of Spies* 《用间篇》
>
> 故唯明君贤将，能以上智为间者，必成大功。
> Therefore, enlightened rulers and good generals who are able to obtain intelligent agents as spies are certain of great achievements.
> — *Chapter: Use of Spies* 《用间篇》

A wise general can always achieve outstanding results and win in battles because of his clear understanding of the enemy. This understanding of the enemy is not through superstitious fortune telling, astrology or listening to rumours. It is achieved through an agent who has insider's information of the enemy.

A wise general will make use of a smart person to gather intelligence. This is an important step in war manoeuvre. How the whole troop advances depends on this intelligence.

An entrepreneur needs to understand the function of intelligence in a competitive business environment. No effort should be spared to gather, analyze and utilize the information. He must stand firm in believing the power of information and quickly take note of the signal of change from the information. Consequently, he needs to make changes to the products and services where necessary to remain in the competitive race.

Case Study 68: Simple Information That Earned USD 25 Million

The chairman of Guang Da Industrial Company in China, Wang Guang Ying knew the importance of business intelligence. Once, he was reading an article and obtained important information.

"Used but reputable industrial vehicles for sale!"

The apparent simple sentence, nonetheless, contained important business intelligence.

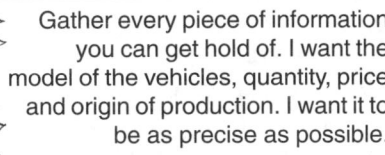

"Gather every piece of information you can get hold of. I want the model of the vehicles, quantity, price and origin of production. I want it to be as precise as possible."

Wang immediately summoned his subordinates to put their acts together.

Very soon, Wang got more details he wanted.

"A large mine in Chile was in financial difficulties. The owner had recently bought a few American "Dodge" and German "Benz" dump trucks. The number of vehicles up for sale was 1,500. To pay the bank debts, the owner had no choice but to sell these new trucks at a discount."

Wang knew that there were other keen buyers from Hong Kong and elsewhere. These buyers, like him, had noticed the deal was good. He immediately assembled his team of taskforce.

You have full authority in negotiation for this deal.

Very quickly, the taskforce arrived in Chile. They carefully inspected the dump trucks.

The conditions of the trucks are good.

An agreement was reached after a few rounds of negotiations with the owner: 1,500 dump trucks would be sold to Guang Da Industrial Company at a discount of 62%. In the deal, Guang Da enjoyed a saving of USD 25 million.

Huge economic returns come after bold actions acted on accurate information and timely analyzed intelligence.

Case Study 69: Good Understanding Of Information In A Successful Negotiation

In early June 1987, the plant manager of Ji Nan Machinery Factory in China, Sun Bao Jun, visited America for a business negotiation. The negotiation with Los Angeles-based Kallman Company, reached a deadlock. It was 9 June 1987. For the ensuing two days, no response was heard from his American partner.

Sun heard this:

The management of Kallman has earlier signed an agreement with some Taiwanese businessmen. The American government has, however, raised taxes on imports from Asian countries like Japan, Korea and Taiwan to protect its trade interests.

With the higher tax, the Taiwanese manufacturers are reluctant to export. In turn, this might cause delay for shipment from Kallman to its own American customers.

Kallman is in a difficult position. The management appears composed on the surface but internally, they are filled with anxieties. The management of Kallman is anxiously studying the quality of Ji Nan's machines. They are in the preparatory stage in signing the purchase agreement. This agreement is their key out of the difficult position.

Sun was calm and waited patiently for the outcome. In due course, Kallman took the initiative to negotiate and reached an agreement with Ji Nan. The agreement was to purchase 150 machines.

Case Study 70: Leverage On Information And Be The First Mover Into A Market

In the 1970s, Korean entrepreneur and founder of Daewoo, Kim Woo-Choong, tried to penetrate into the American textile market. Daewoo then had already earned USD 18 million a year by exporting men's wear.

"We must develop a new market."

"We need to be careful of the changes."

In 1971, there was a rumour that America would adopt a quota system for textile imports. Many exporters adopted a wait-and-see attitude. The textile manufacturers reduced their export to America and seek new markets elsewhere.

"The quota system in America is based on trade data from the previous year. The approved quota for the year will depend on the import quantity of the previous year. The larger the import the previous year, the larger the quota allocated for the year."

Kim received this essential piece of information.

"Let's work and make sure that we increase export into the American market for the remaining of this year."

Kim was certain in his objective.

In 1972, Daewoo was given the biggest share in import quota to US among all Asian textile exporters. That year alone, the export of Daewoo's high-end men's wear hit record numbers and Kim was the "undisputed winner in America's textile quota system".

With a higher export quota into America, Kim also convinced the store chain with 900 department stores to sell his men's wear. Daewoo became the first Korean company to have a direct trade co-operation with an American company. This set the precedence of doing away with the middleman role of Japanese trading house for trade between Korea and America.

In November 1981, Kim was recognized by the Korean government for his "achievement in foreign trade of USD 1.5 billion".

America's restrictive quota system was a nightmare for many textile makers, but it turned out to be a triumph for Daewoo. Kim was able to pore over the finer details of the system and made his moves before the other exporters. His action won him a glorious victory.

Market and Information Analysis

Section 2 Analyze the environment and know your competitors

> 知己知彼，百战不殆；不知彼而知己，一胜一负；不知彼不知己，每战必殆。
> One who knows the enemy and knows himself will not be in danger in a hundred battles.
> One who does not know the enemy but knows himself will sometimes win, sometimes lose.
> One who does not know the enemy and does not know himself will be in danger in every battle.
>
> — Chapter: Attack by Stratagem 《谋攻篇》

Know your enemy and yourself to emerge safe from danger in each battle. Know only yourself and not the enemy may lead to either a victory or a defeat. Neither knowing your enemy nor yourself would be dangerous in all battles.

In management, "knowing others" refers to knowing the market changes, transformation in consumers' psychology and situation of the competitors. It also includes information on structural changes in politics and economics where the business is operating in.

"Knowing oneself" encompasses knowledge of one's company and the situation surrounding you. There is a Chinese proverb "当局者迷" (English translation: "A spectator sees more than a player in the heat of a game.") which collaterally explained that "knowing oneself" is not easily achieved. We need to be objective and scientific when we attempt to understand ourselves.

Today, business is conducted in an international setting, hence the entrepreneur needs to be aware of the changes in the regional politics and economics. The business is also affected by differences in regional customs and traditions. The entrepreneur must be quick in recognizing the differences and changes to make a correct decision.

Case Study 71: Understand The Market And Ascertain The Direction

Japanese entrepreneur, Kiichiro Toyoda, chose car manufacturing as his business. His first task was a study tour around the world to learn about the industry and the market. Between 1929 and 1930, Kiichiro visited many cities of the Western countries. He was particularly impressed by the German automaker, Mercedez Benz and the American automaker, Ford.

A glorious era for automobile in human history will soon dawn.

The two-year study tour made him realize that a large gap existed between Japanese and Western automakers. It also confirmed his belief in the bright future of the automobile market. He was adamant to make his car manufacturing business a success.

The success of the Japanese automobile industry depends on talents. After my study tour, I will make all efforts to attract talented people and their support.

Kiichiro made this important remark while concluding his tour.

With the help of many professionals, Kiichiro established a supply base of quality gear-systems using superior steel.

Kiichiro Toyoda acknowledged the suggestions of experts and combined the merits in design and manufacturing of auto brand names like Ford and Chevrolet. Toyota designed its own flagship models of cars that were "fuel-saving, robust and inexpensive".

In 1938, Toyota car plant went into production. By 1948, Toyota was producing small saloon cars. Today, Toyota produces 3 million cars per year, dominating one-tenth of the world's automobile production.

Success comes from a broad-based investigation and profound understanding of the gap with competitors. The understanding ascertains the direction for enterprise management and market trend. In this case, one will not be left in a passive mode.

Case Study 72: Cheers From Customers For The Melodic Tune

Before 1981, Pearl River Piano, manufactured by Guang Zhou Piano Factory, was the least well-known in China among the four local piano makers. In 1984, the piano won the "Golden Dragon Award" for its quality in tone and sound at the China Piano Appraisal.

"The quality of Pearl River Piano is comparable to the branded pianos made in Germany."

Chinese celebrated pianists, Liu Shi Kun and Yin Cheng Zong gave these compliments after they played their pieces on the piano.

The factory manager summarized the winning strategy as "knowing oneself and knowing the competitors".

200 million homes

200,000 sets

"Knowing the competitors" is to recognize the market situation. We thoroughly studied the piano market and realized that we were not up to mark even for the local market. We estimated there are a total of 200 million homes and each family consists of five members. With a penetration rate of 1/1000 for pianos into these families, simple math tells us the local market size is at least 200,000.

There are more than half a million schools and nurseries in China. If half this number of schools were to buy a piano for their students, this segment of market is 250,000. The combined market size for these two segments gives a total of 450,000 potential buyers. The piano market indeed has huge potential.

500,000 schools

250,000 sets

"Knowing oneself" is to understand the level of technology, the condition of production facility and the quality of employees of the company.

To manufacture a piano with acceptable quality, the piano needs to have a refined finishing and be able to produce crystal clear sounds. The whole piano manufacturing process consists of 51 steps; involving 580 types of materials and more than 8,000 parts for assembly. It would be impossible to make a good piano without the necessary technology and facility.

The company recognized its own weaknesses and made every attempt to improve technology know-how and workers' expertise. It overcame many technical difficulties in the manufacturing processes. The quality of the product improved dramatically ever since.

50,000 sets

20,000 sets

10,000 sets

1985   1987   1990

Market for pianos

One must pay attention to the market to understand business conditions. Conducting market research and site observation provide clear understanding of the business situation. The management requires this knowledge to reach out to the customers and market.

Case Study 73: The Failure In Development Of The Edsel Saloon Car

1/5 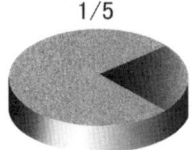   1/3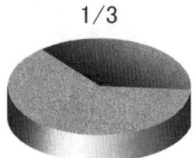

The market for mid-range cars had a sustained growth at the beginning of the 20th century. The demand for these cars grew from one-fifth of the market to more than one-third of the market by middle of the 1950s.

However, the mid-range cars had always been a weak link in Ford automobiles. There was only one Ford model competing with other makers' models. The model took up 20% of Ford's manufacturing capacity.

To improve the mid-range market share, Ford introduced the Edsel saloon in 1957. The objective was to at least achieve 3.3% to 3.5% of America's total car market. Ford spent a lot of money and resources to reach the objective.

Three versions of Edsel saloon were introduced in the ensuing years. The market was not enthusiastic with these models. Edsel saloon was taken off from production and out of competition due to poor market response in 1959. How could a product that had gone through thorough planning and resource allocation turn out to be a failure? Whatever happened to the years of market experience in managing new products?

There were many reasons: Edsel saloon was introduced at a time when the American economy was in recession. The market segment that was most badly affected then was the mid-range car market.

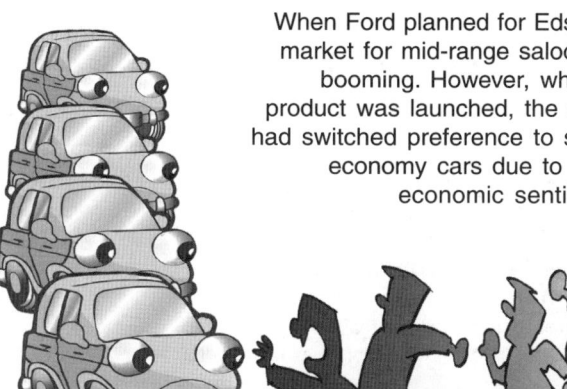

When Ford planned for Edsel, the market for mid-range saloon was booming. However, when the product was launched, the market had switched preference to smaller economy cars due to poorer economic sentiments.

The whole project for Edsel took a number of years from product planning to product introduction. The design team overlooked the possibility of changes in consumers' preference. The introduction was further battered by the newly enacted law introduced by the American Transport Department. This law forbade mentioning of a car's engine size and speed in advertisement. These two features, apparently, were the performing attributes of Edsel.

The market's preference for smaller and simple cars also worked against the flashy design of Edsel. The customers hence rejected Ford's effort in Edsel.

Failure in product research and development stems from a misjudgment of market changes and a constricted view of the economic conditions, competitors and consumers' preference. These misunderstandings can result in expensive investment and heavy losses.

Market and Information Analysis

Section 3 Analyze the overall market scientifically and accurately

> 兵法：一曰度，二曰量，三曰数，四曰称，五曰胜。地生度，度生量，量生数，数生称，称生胜。
> The factors in warfare are:
> First: scope, second: quantity, third: number, fourth: comparison, and fifth: victory.
> Scopes are derived from the ground,
> quantities are derived from measurement,
> numbers are derived from quantities,
> comparisons are derived from calculations,
> and victories are derived from comparisons.
> — Chapter: *Use of Military Momentum* 《行军篇》
>
> 地形有通者、有挂者、有支者、有隘者、有险者、有远者
> 凡此六者，地之道也，将之至任，不可不察也。
> The grounds are accessible, entrapping, stalemated, narrow, steep, and expansive. These six situations are not caused by heaven or earth, but by the general.
> — Chapter: *The Terrain* 《地形篇》

There are five principles in assessing terrain in the Art of War. "Scope" refers to the size of the battleground that depends on the terrain of the battlefield. "Quantity" — how large is the battle. "Number" — the number of troops in the battle. "Comparison" — balance of power in military strength. Hence, through the knowledge of size of the battleground we determine the number of troops; through the number of troops, we determine the strength and finally through the strength of the troops we determine the eventual winner.

To determine the outcome of the battle, we need to make a comparative study of the battle terrain, size and strength of the fighting troops to make an overall analysis.

The principles for assessing terrain can be similarly applied to the analysis of business competition and market.

On a more specific account: 1. Scope — accurate judgment on the size of total market in a specific period of sales for the whole industry. 2. Quantity — the realizable market demand. 3. Number — A measure of the resource allocation capability and how much resources the competitors are able to mobilize to enter a new market. 4. Weight — An accurate measure of competitors' strengths and weaknesses. 5. Victory — the selection of an appropriate strategy and course of action according to the market characteristics and relative strengths. The entrepreneur needs to adopt the most suitable competitive strategy while having a full understanding of the whole market. This is done through a scientific analysis of the market information.

The correct use of principles requires one to be accurate and scientific.

Case Study 74: A Small Plant Can Also Find Its Advantage

Ping Lu Axial Manufacturing from Shanxi province, China, was a small machinery plant. Its axial shaft products were used in many engineering applications. The plant was in a remote area, located far from the provincial city. The company was in financial difficulties after sales dropped in 1980. In 1987, Wu, was appointed as the new plant manager. Wu studied more than 100 other manufacturers of machinery axial shafts and the market. He also analyzed his plant's capability and product.

> There are many competitors in the market. Our products are old and not competitive.

> The government has slowed down on infrastructure construction and there is a decrease in the use of engineering equipment. Our inventory is accumulating.

The railway has traditionally been the pillar in China's transport industry. The industry is in its crucial stage of growth and the demand for electric generators for railroads is growing. The market for axial shafts used in electric generators is potentially huge.

"The factory of Ping Lu Axial Manufacturing is located close to the makers of electric generators. The proximity to customers is an advantage."

"There are only eight manufacturers of axial shaft for electric generators. As long as the toughness of our axial shaft satisfies the requirement, we have confidence in penetrating the market."

"To move out from the financial difficulty, we must create new and innovative products. From the analysis, I have decided to make axial shafts for generators our strategic product."

After two years of earnest efforts, Ping Lu Axial Manufacturing became the designated supplier for a main maker of electric generator, Yong Ji Electric. It also established a supply relationship with more than 40 other railroad contractors. Ping Lu Axial Manufacturing's market share for axial shaft steadily grew to 60 percent.

All companies, big or small, can always acquire a competitive edge for success with accurate forecast. We can make use of the advances in computer technology to establish an information management system that greatly helps the company.

Case Study 75: Success Secret Of The King Of Fastener

The founder of YKK fastener products, Yoshida Tadao, said the following of his company's success: Adjust the sales strategy according to overseas demand.

Since the 1980s, the expansion into foreign market has increased with the economic might of Japan. Trade war with the Western countries was obvious on account of more trade barriers established by the Europeans and Americans. Yoshida had earlier noticed the changes taking place in the overseas market in the 1970s. He also realized the savings potential in production cost and raw materials for overseas production sites. The on-going trade war greatly encouraged foreign investments in the local economy to reduce reliance on imports.

Yoshida decided to produce and sell locally. YKK was able to overcome the trade barriers and lower production cost. The company was successful and made a handsome profit.

Through a chain reaction that was set up positively, YKK was able to move ahead in the competition. In its expansion into foreign markets, YKK adopted a price reduction strategy that took away some profitability but effectively attracted customers. This strategy was a huge blow to its competitors.

A company needs to make money but it does not need to take up all the profits. We can divide "profit" into three portions: One portion is the value for customers. The second portion is the share for agents and distributors. The last portion is profit for the company.

At YKK factory, you can hardly find a machine that is three years or older.

Improve the product quality. An inexpensive product must be accompanied by good quality. YKK relentlessly upgraded the equipment and improved its processes. To achieve this, YKK produced many new equipment each year for their licensed makers worldwide. They helped them renew their equipment, ensuring that their production facilities were always in the best condition.

Modernize production and maintain a high level of automation. To engage our competitors, YKK constantly enhances its production facilities. Since 1965, YKK has constantly offered many new fastener products but the production cost has decreased by half.

The success of YKK lies in its ability to accurately analyze similar products' "scope", "quantity", "number" and further make "comparison" found in the international market. A tailored strategy that circumvented the competitive barriers and lowered cost of production helped strengthen the company's level of technology and product quality.

Case Study 76: Cause Of Failure — Inflexibility

The Rayly's bicycle company of Britain was established in 1887. Durability had always been the maxim in production. A Rayly bicycle is still good after 60 to 70 years of use. A Rayly bicycle is well known for its reliability and quality. The demand for Rayly's bicycle was strong worldwide.

The beginning of the 1960s saw automobiles transforming into an integral part of European families. Consequently, the sales of bicycle dropped. Rayly's doggedly believed that bicycles would still represent the main mode of transport in the future. It was until 1977 that the company decided to make changes when survivability became an issue.

The Asian bicycle manufacturers penetrated the European market with lower price and better marketing strategies in the 1980s.

The Taiwanese manufacturers and American distributors worked together and sold the Taiwan-made bicycle under the American distributors' brand name. The alliance was successful in the American market and saved on advertising cost. The bicycles were also sold at a lower price while quality had not been compromised.

By 1986, the sales had reached 5.6 million. Rayly's bicycles were priced out of the European and American markets. It later lost its market share in the African and Asian markets.

In 1982, Rayly's bicycle could not pull itself out from its financial crunch and was acquired by British Dolby Company. In 1986, the number of employees was reduced from 10,000 to 1,700. Even with the big cut in headcounts, the losses that year still amounted to USD 9.6 million.

Retrenched 8,300 workers
Total losses USD 9.6 million

In business competition, one must be sharp to identify the opportunity, understand the changes and secure the existing market. Taking a step further, select the right opportunity for attack and improve the market share. Conformance to the old and proven way, without flexible responses to changing market needs will lead to a breakdown in operations.

Chapter 8
Business Competition

Section 1 Seize the business opportunity

Section 2 Looking for the best returns

Section 3 Dealing with uncertainties

Business Competition

Section 1　Seize the business opportunity

> 故兵贵胜，不贵久。
> The important thing in doing battle is victory, not protracted warfare.
> 　　　　　　　　　　　　— *Chapter: Waging War* 《作战篇》
>
> 兵之情主速，乘人之不及。由不虞之道，攻其所不戒也。
> To take advantage of the enemy's lack of preparation, take unexpected routes to attack where the enemy is not prepared.
> 　　　　　　　　　— *Chapter: Nine Types of Strategic Grounds* 《九地篇》

To fight in a war is to win a quick and decisive battle. A quick attack on the enemy will catch them off-guard. Travel the least expected route and attack where the defence is the slackest.

Sunzi's Art of War advocated a quick and decisive battle and strongly opposed a prolonged war. Procrastination and indecisive command exhaust valuable resources and will waste strategic advantages. A quick and sudden attack will catch the enemy off-guard. Applying this war philosophy to business would mean to be quick in seizing the business opportunity.

For an entrepreneur, time is both money and the essence.

1. Business opportunities come and go in succession. They may not appear twice. The person who captures the opportunity will gain the upperhand and could move by leaps and bounds. The person who loses the opportunity will be put in a state of defence and may eventually lose.
2. An increase in productivity means better use of time. Without additional investment or expansion in production, there will still be increased output.
3. The pace of activities in today's business environment has increased dramatically. This is applicable to all areas of business, which include new product development, new product introduction, sales and marketing, after-sales services, corporate communication and advertising. Whoever seizes the opportunity seizes the day.

Seize the business opportunity and win a decisive battle!

Case Study 77: Speed — The Battle Between Life And Death Of A Company

In 1979, China exported 3,000 tons of walnuts to East Germany (formerly the Federal Republic of Germany). The contract of supply stated: the walnuts have to be on supermarket shelves by 4 December, in time for the high demand on St Nicholas Day. Unfortunately, the containers only reached the port in end November.

The port workers are resting today. The goods can only be unloaded the following Monday. The entire shipment of walnuts takes six days to unload.

That is a pity!

The Chinese exporters missed an opportunity for good sales by a couple of days. The quick-witted American exporters were there to seize the market.

There is strong demand for gold plated necklaces at the "Trade Show for Tourism Souvenirs". The trade show is scheduled to start on 3 October 1979 in Gui Yang.

On 29 September 1979, Fujian Mi Hou Handicraft Factory's plant manager, Wan Guan Hua, heard of the exhibition. He organised his technicians to work on the products and chose 37 exquisite necklaces for the trade show.

Within a few days, the factory received many orders. Wan brought more samples to other trade shows and he received more orders. From the orders in the trade shows, he managed to bring his company to greater heights.

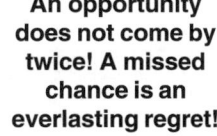

An opportunity does not come by twice! A missed chance is an everlasting regret!

Case Study 78: A Timely Purchase

In the autumn of 1984, former East German Automaker, Zundapp, announced its closure and was putting the factory up for sale. A city official from Tianjin heard of the sale and reported it to his office.

Zündapp is more than 67 years old and is well equipped with the latest automobile technology. It has a big market share in Europe. We should consider buying the company.

There were other parties from India and Iran who were interested in buying the automobile maker. The Iranians acted fast to sign a purchase agreement with the Germans, which stated the payment amount and realization date.

The deadline is 24 October 1984 3.00 pm.

Officials from Tianjin responded immediately.

As long as the deal is not sealed, we can make our bid.

On 22 October, Tianjin officials organized a mission to Germany to discuss on the deal. By 23 October, the officials were in Munich for discussion.

The officials worked hard to gather information.

The opportunity is here!

On 24 October, the agreed payment terms by the Iranians to the Germans did not materialize. They requested for an extension.

Case Study 79: Continuous Innovation Of Products

In June 1988, the Tam brothers from Hong Kong, Samson and Thomas, established Group Sense Limited (GSL). They got their business idea from the English electronic dictionary that had become very popular in America.

The electronic dictionary is compact and useful. If we are able to produce a Chinese-English electronic dictionary in Hong Kong, we will be the pioneer in the Chinese electronics dictionary. There is a big market waiting for us.

After nine months of continuous effort, the first Chinese-English dictionary — INSTANT-DIC EC1000 — made its debut. In a short period of 10 months, more than 100,000 electronic dictionaries were sold. In 1990, the Tam brothers established a manufacturing plant at Bo An in Shenzhen and began marketing INSTANT-DIC.

The Tam brothers' success attracted attention from other electronic makers and many similar products began to flood the market. An intense competition ensued.

We need to innovate continuously so as to maintain our leadership.

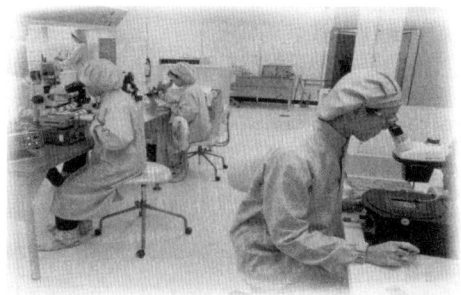

GSL maintained its technological superiority by working closely with research institutes and universities in Hong Kong. The researchers of GSL were keen to learn the latest technological advancement.

The use of multiple avenues for research and development allowed GSL to introduce new products faster than its competitors.

The Tam brothers worked hard to develop a full sentence translator that was smarter than the existing single word translator. This new product was to be its differentiating factor.

In 1991, Thomas Tam noticed that scientists at the Chinese Academy of Sciences successfully developed an artificial intelligent translator. He made a business trip to Beijing and discussed a possible collaboration with the academy.

Making use of logic-reasoning, the world's first English-to-Chinese full-sentence translator, **EC863A, was developed.** Product innovation has enabled GSL to become a leader.

Business Competition

Section 2   Looking for the best returns

> 故兵以诈立，以利动……
> The army is established on deception, mobilized by advantage…..
> — *Chapter: Manoeuvring*　《军争篇》
>
> 掠乡分众，廓地分利，悬权而动。
> When you plunder the countryside, divide the wealth among your troops;
> When you expand your territory, divide up and hold places of advantage.
> — *Chapter: Manoeuvring*　《军争篇》

A changing strategy needs to be adopted to win a battle and risk calculation must be made to decide on the course of action. After plundering a village, there will be wealth to be divided, prisoners to be taken and land to be shared. A calculation needs to be done for allocation purposes.

In the battle, the manoeuvres are dependent on the costs and benefits. This cost and benefits calculation had always been the central analysis in Sunzi's decision. The ultimate objective of a war is to annihilate and conquer the enemies. Hence, the opponents in a battle will seek the most beneficial approach. Once an opportunity arises, decisive action needs to be taken. It can be said that the cause of a war is the result of a tussle over the potential benefit for the victor. The amount of benefit will decide the size of the battle. On the same note, in a competitive business, an entrepreneur needs to bear in mind that reaping the most benefits is of utmost importance. It is a guiding principle in running a business.

Case Study 80: Purchase Of Alaska For USD 7.2 Million

Alaska is located in the bitterly cold north-west corner of North America. It was previously a Russian territory. The Russians decided to sell the arctic territory and negotiated with the Americans. The agreement, widely referred to as "Seward's Folly" (and "Seward's Icebox") ceded possession of the vast territory of Alaska to the United States for the sum of USD 7.2 million. Alaska became the 49th state of America.

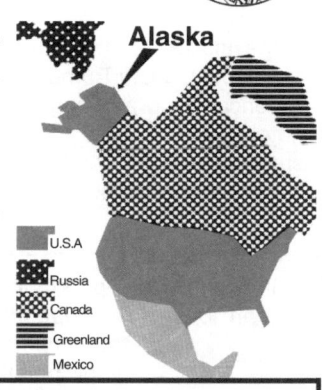

"A black sheep!"

The American civil war had just ended. Few citizens of the U.S. could fathom what possible use or interest the 586,000 square miles of land would have for their country. Many congressmen also directed their objection at then Secretary of State William H. Seward for this decision.

We should think beyond the current situation. There will be long-term benefits and this is a God-sent opportunity. If the Russians were to sell this piece of land to another country, we would be the ones lamenting.

Not long after Russia ceded possession of the territory, gold was found on this abandoned land. In the 20th century, the biggest oil reserve in North America was found and Alaska is still producing, till today, one-seventh of America's total oil production.

Seward finally convinced the Congress of the purchase.

Comparatively speaking, incisive observation and strategic vision are needed to achieve long-term benefits.

Case Study 81: Capital-Free Investment In Property Boom

In the mid 1970s, American real estate developer Donald Trump heard that Pan American Railway wanted to sell an old hotel building located at the central station. The hotel location was good and it seemed to have good potential.

"It is an old building. I am willing to pay USD 10 million for it. I will place USD 250,000 as downpayment."

Trump seized the opportunity and began lobbying for support from treasury officials in his purchase.

"I am inking a big tax-free deal with the City Council. If the bank is not going to provide the loan, it will be your greatest regret."

He went on to convince the bankers.

The New York City government was running a tight budget and agreed to the deal. Trump obtained the biggest property tax exemption in New York City and also inked a loan of USD 80 million from the bank.

The hotel underwent a major facelift and Trump put his name on it. Trump, however, did not spend a penny on it. According to federal tax regulation, the annual estate tax for the hotel was supposed to be USD 9 million. In the period of the major facelift, Trump had saved USD 350 million. The property prices soared once the hotel reopened. By 1987, the daily room rate for the hotel was USD 200 and the hotel made an annual profit of USD 35 million.

> Putting up a deceptive smoke screen is part of an overall enterprise strategy. There is no point for an all-out crash with the opponent if one wishes to reap the most benefit with the least cost. It is more important to adopt an indirect tactic in public relations to pitch for the opponent's favour and make him slacken his guard. This helps to create advantageous opportunity and benefits for the enterprise.

Case Study 82: Manage According to Profitability

Li Zhi Company and Hua Ying Company each built a shopping arcade on both sides of a busy road in downtown Hong Kong.

Between the two companies, Li Zhi is financially stronger.

The Chairman of Hua Ying, Mr Lin An, knew of the financial disparity between the two companies.

Li Zhi is targeting the upmarket shoppers. In that case, we will not compete directly with them. We will target the middle and low range market.

Li Zhi Company is in a financial squeeze and has to turn its market strategy to focus on the lower tier market.

Two months into the construction of the shopping arcade, bad news came.

The construction of our shopping arcade is in its final phase too. If we are to follow the original plan, we will clash head on and we will be at the losing end. We should look into other possibilities.

The shopping arcades were located in a business district and there were many high-class restaurants. Restaurants and eateries catering to the working people were few and the existing ones seemed to be doing well. In particular a Si Chuan cuisine eatery was extremely popular.

There is high human traffic here and many of the customers are workers. There are also rich and famous people who visit us for our authentic dishes.

How about transforming the arcade into a food square that specializes in mainland Chinese dishes? We could hire Chinese chefs to cook these authentic dishes.

All we need is to add a kitchen facility and we will be ready for business.

Hua Ying transformed the arcade into a food square. After the food square was opened, it was filled with eager diners. At the close of the year, Hua Ying's profit was 30% higher than Li Zhi's.

Thinking of the possible outcomes before embarking on a business is the key to success.

Business Competition
Section 3 Dealing with uncertainties

> 夫兵形象水，水之行避高而趋下，兵之形避实而击虚；水因地而制流，
> 兵因敌而制胜。故兵无常势，水无常形。能因敌变化而取胜者，谓之神。
> — *Chapter: Weaknesses and strengths* 《虚实篇》
>
> The army's formation is like water.
> The water's formation avoids the high and rushes to the low.
> So an army's formation avoids the strong and rushes to the weak.
> The water's formation adapts to the ground when flowing.
> So then an army's formation adapts to the enemy to achieve victory.
> Therefore, an army does not have constant force, or have constant formation.
> Those who are able to adapt and change in accord with the enemy and achieve victory are called divine.

The manoeuvre of troops is like the water flowing from high ground to low ground. Likewise in battle formation, we avoid the enemy's vantage point and attack its weaknesses.

The flow of water depends on the gradient of the ground while the formation of a battle depends on the enemy's course of action. There is no fixed law in the conduct of battle. An adept army is one that wins a battle by out-manoeuvring the enemy.

A small scale production would look to stay firm on its course with no change. The current management practice suggests the contrary. The message is "to look for small changes and achieve perfection through them". Competition is continuous and situations vary accordingly. An adept entrepreneur is able to sense minor signals of change and make the necessary adjustment to create a more advantageous situation for the organization. In today's business environment, there is no certainty of everlasting superiority. It is definitely not a time to let your guard down.

Case Study 83: Playing To Score And Winning By Surprise

In 1950, Li Ka-Shing and his partners came up with HKD 50,000 to start Cheung Kong Rubber Factory. The business was not doing well for a couple of years.

Li Ka-Shing analyzed the situation and found that some Italian companies were making plastic flowers and selling to the Americans for a very good profit. He immediately went to Italy to learn the techniques for making plastic flowers.

After learning the skill of making plastic flowers, Li transformed Cheung Kong into a factory producing plastic flowers. While many people were unconvinced of the market potential, Li's business grew with many overseas orders. He was soon crowned the "king of plastic flowers". Li went on to look for more opportunities.

The plastic flower industry was declining and there were limited business opportunities. Many smaller companies entered into the crowded industry. Li, by then had moved into properties. That was in 1958.

By 1964, the plastic flower industry in Hong Kong had withered. In 1967, there was a property glut where properties were sold cheaply in Hong Kong.

Li picked the right moment and started to buy properties to build his estate empire.

In 1972, he looked for extra capital in the capital market. This further increased the financial strength of Cheung Kong and he started buying into other businesses. His quick-witted business manoeuvres and ability to sniff out good opportunities kept him away from bad investments. Today, he has transformed Cheung Kong into one of Hong Kong's largest companies.

In 1997, Li proved himself as a maestro of business deals by investing into China.

Time the changes and react with the necessary strategy to market conditions. Initiative is an important factor of success for a company.

Case Study 84: Changing The Production From Soft Tubes To Toothpaste

Guang Zhou Tubing Company was the only manufacturer of toothpaste tubes and medicine tubes. The company's tubes were in high demand. The mid 1970s marked a period of dynamic development for the plastic industry in China. Plastic tubes substituted metallic tubes as the packaging material for toothpaste. There was also keen competition.

They company noticed that the market for conventional toothpaste was saturated. There was an emerging market for Chinese herbal toothpaste. The management decided to produce herbal toothpaste.

The company worked with First Army Medical University and came up with the best ingredients for the toothpaste. The herbal toothpaste was known as "Jie Ying". In 1982, "Jie Ying" toothpaste was on sale. The consumers responded positively to the product. The company sold more than 2 million Jie Ying toothpaste within six months.

To make the presence of its fledging product felt in other places of China and overseas, the company adopted an aggressive advertisement campaign for Jie Ying.

In 1983, the order for soft tubes decreased by one-fifth that of 1981. On the contrary, the production of toothpaste increased by eight folds as compared to 1982.

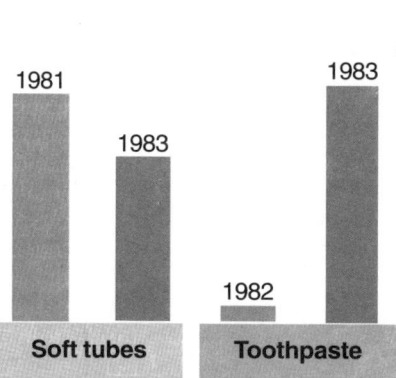

The company's transformation is rooted to the changes and necessities of the market. It is done through research & development effort for new products that create and satisfy new demands. With new markets developed, the company is able to stand the test in dynamic market conditions.

Case Study 85: Factory On A Ship

In 1864, Alfred Nobel used his patent in nitroglycerine (blasting oil) as an industrial explosive. He set up the first company in the world that manufactured explosives. At that time, people were not familiar with the chemical properties and safety precautions needed for this newfound technology. Accidents were commonplace. Alfred Nobel's younger brother, Emil, was killed while preparing nitroglycerine at Heleneborg, Stockholm. The Stockholmers were worried about this new technology and refused to lease a factory space to them. Alfred Nobel was in a difficult position.

If the factory were to be located in a remote place, the transportation cost would be exorbitant. Besides, there was no guarantee that accidents would not happen during transportation. Nobel came up with an idea.

Stockholm is located at the western bank of the Gulf of Bothnia, situated at the entrance of Lake Maleran. The water channel is wide and there are many small islets.

Alfred Nobel used the geographical landscape as a natural explosion barrier and bought a barge to be used as the production factory. His barge-factory was anchored away from the crowded city. With this "factory site", Nobel was able to silence his critics and reduce the transportation cost and risk.

Nobel's ingenious solution made his explosive business possible. This in turn formed the foundation for future expansion of his business. He thought out-of-the-box and cleverly used the physical environment to solve his problem. Many other examples have shown that unorthodox ideas can turn an impossibility into reality.

Chapter 9
Art of Establishing Business Relationship and Negotiation

Section 1 Negotiation is an important technique in business

Section 2 The techniques of negotiation

Art of Establishing Business Relationship and Negotiation

Section 1 Negotiation is an important technique in business

> 故上兵伐谋，其次伐交，其次伐兵，其下攻城。
> The best warfare strategy is to attack the enemy's plans, next is to attack alliances, then attack the army, and the last is to attack a walled city.
> — *Chapter: Attack by Stratagem* 《谋攻篇》

The best strategy is to thwart the enemy's battle plan. The second best is to foil the enemy's diplomacy. The third best is to win the enemy's troops. The worst is to attack the enemy's fortress.

Diplomacy and negotiation are more important means than direct engagement in a battle. This is an important philosophy in Sunzi's Art of War. Sunzi treated diplomatic negotiation as an integral part of assessing the situation. He believed that to win without a fight is the most intelligent manoeuvre in a battle strategy. In the heat of business competition, the company needs to outperform competitors on product quality, product variety, price and services. Besides these performance attributes, the enterprise needs to reckon the importance of business relationship and negotiation.

The diplomatic activities of an enterprise refer primarily to negotiation. It is one of the most important activities of a business operator but is often overlooked by many. Business negotiation is concerned with the products (or technology and services) and terms of agreement that will eventually produce a successful business deal. It is also the process that moves from divergence in opinion to convergence in thinking.

An experienced entrepreneur will use his intelligence, astuteness and patience to negotiate for a common goal with his counterpart. This is the highest realm in negotiation.

Case Study 86: Negotiate On Facts

In the 1970s, Chinese Civil Aviation bought Fokker planes and more than 100 SPEY engines from a British manufacturer. After almost 10 years in operation, these engines began to show significant signs of problems in the 1980s.

A maintenance engineer of Chinese Civil Aviation, Xue Qi Zhu, diagnosed and discovered that the cause was vibration in the engines. She made a claim against the British manufacturer.

The problems are caused by the engine vibration and the British should pay for the damages.

The British did not accept the allegation and proposed otherwise.

The company has already solved the inherent vibration problem of the engine in the '60s. The original SPEY engine has been improved. This improvement is known as 2848 modification. The purchase documents have specified that the SPEY engines the Chinese have purchased are modified versions. The company guarantees that there is no problem with the engines.

Xue began his further investigation to clarify the disagreement. On 8 September 1984, Xue represented Chinese Civilian Aviation in its claim against the British. At the negotiation, She presented large amounts of data and documented materials.

During my supervision of two SPEY engines repair work at the British manufacturing plant, I had a conversation with the chief inspector. I had to give sufficient evidence of a direct relationship between the vibration problem and the components used.

I have discovered old components used before the 2848 modification from the dismantled engine.

The British mentioned that there is a need to increase the thickness of the fifth blade in the engine. If modification 2848 has been made to the engine, why is there necessity to increase the blade thickness?

We have strong reasons to believe that you have installed defective blades into engines sold to foreign buyers except those for British Airways. This is despite the fact that we have made payment for the modified designs. This is an intentional transfer of losses to customers.

Know oneself, know the enemy. It is a maxim that applies in all conflicts, be it at war or otherwise. It is the most important element for success and essence in negotiation. We need to work hard to discover the opponent's weaknesses and attack them. "Attack when the other is unprepared, attack where least expected."

Case Study 87: Looking For Death Spot Of Opponent In Negotiation

In the 1970s, the Chinese spent more than RMB 1 billion to purchase three chemical fertilizer production facilities. These facilities were installed in Nanjing, Guangzhou and Anqing. During the test operation, the turbo machinery at Nanjing experienced three instances of crack at the rotary blades. Each of these instances resulted in losses of more than RMB 45,000. The engineers and experts of both buyer and seller disagreed on who should bear the losses. The foreign experts maintained that the Chinese were responsible.

The cracks occurred by chance. The economic losses should be borne by the Chinese.

After our detailed analysis, the problem was concluded to be caused by excessive vibration and insufficient factor of safety in vibration index for design. This is a design issue. We have valid reasons to request for a replacement and payment for losses.

Chinese Professor Meng Qing Ji expressed his opinion.

The economic loss is big and is difficult for compensation. Our product design strictly follows the design theory proposed by world renowned turbo machinery expert, German Professor Walter Traupel.

Case Study 88: Patience Is The Essence Of Negotiation

Jim was the founder of an American software company. He was in Japan to negotiate with a Japanese computer manufacturer. He arrived in Tokyo one day earlier as he was anxious to close the deal.

The next day, Jim arrived at the reception of Yamada's office. The anxiety in his mind was nowhere to hide.

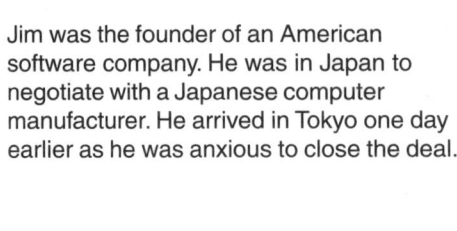

If I am successful in the negotiation, we can increase the annual sales three folds. This is important!!

After 15 minutes' wait at the reception, he was invited into Yamada's office. The two men exchanged greetings and business cards. Jim immediately put the business card into his pocket and earnestly gestured to start discussion.

Yamada took his time to study Jim's business card.

Have a cup of tea, Mr Jim.

Thank you but it is not necessary…

Allow me to explain our new database management software! It is…

Case Study 89: Negotiation, Sincerity and Co-operation

China First Automotive Works was a manufacturer of trucks. To prepare for its passenger car production, the company sent a team on a study tour to Chrysler in Detroit, the automobile capital of America. The two parties negotiated an initial agreement.

First Automotive will import Chrysler's small saloon car engine and its body frame.

First Automotive representatives made a second visit to realize the agreement. Chrysler had this new information.

The Chinese government has approved China First Automotive's plan to manufacture passenger cars. First Automotive will certainly accede to all conditions as it is a firm decision from the government. Moreover, without the technology transfer from Chrysler, there is no way the Chinese can carry on with the project.

At the second round of negotiation, Chrysler laid down harsh conditions and asked for a very expensive technology transfer fee. The clauses were unfair and First Automotive was not ready to accept the conditions. The management decided that there were other international partners who would be willing to work on a fairer co-operation. The representatives of China First Automotive terminated the discussion and returned to China.

Not long after, the president of Germany's Volkswagen made a courtesy visit to First Automotive. First Automotive realized that Volkswagen was looking for a partner for co-operation. Both parties saw sincerity in co-operation.

We are willing to cooperate with China First Automotive. This will set a good model for co-operation for both parties in future. We are most glad to receive your plant manager in Volkswagen four weeks later.

Four weeks passed. First Automotive's plant manager and his staff visited Volkswagen. The Germans had especially installed a Chrysler engine into the body frame of an Audi for the visit.

The body of the car was purposely lengthened to accommodate the engine.

If China First Automotive is willing to continue working with us, we are willing to accept only USD 1 as symbolic technology transfer fee…

Chrysler was feeling the pressure from Volkswagen. They made an alternative proposal. It was, however, too late.

"Know oneself, know the enemy" helps us to make the correct decision. Through negotiation, observation, comparison, judgment and careful planning, we can know the different attitudes and intent of our potential partners. The sincere partner can thus be identified.

Case Study 90: Taking A Step Back For Long-Term Progress

In 1952, Japanese Matsushita Electric was in a discussion with Philips Electronics on the possibility of technology co-operation. Matsushita Konosuke was successful in negotiating for a lower patent licensing charge of 4.5 percent. This licensing charge does not come easy but after much deliberation.

"The fees for technology transfer will be 7% of gross sales."

"Let's set the licensing fee at 4.5%."

As a clause for lowering the licensing fee, Philips proposed a further condition. The cost of patent transfer will be a lump sum payment of JPY 200 million.

The total capital of Matsushita Electric was less than JPY 500 million at that time. JPY 200 million was a huge amount for the company to bear. The contract was drafted by Philips and hence the penalty for breach of contract was grossly in Philips' favour. Matsushita Konosuke was initially hesitant on the licensing agreement. He was pondering over and over again. The situation was extremely unfavourable for Matsushita on the surface.

"If we take a step back and make some compromises now, it may be good for the company's development. It may also bring benefits for the Japanese electronics industry."

Matsushita wanted a successful technology transfer and co-operation with Philips. He studied the background of Philips in detail. He learnt that Philips had more than 3,000 researchers in its laboratories. These laboratories were well equipped and managed by talented people. These people constantly worked on new developments and innovations.

To build a research centre of this capacity needs billions of Yen and many years. A transfer fee of JPY 200 million definitely paled in comparison to the benefits we get for the access to the talented people and advanced technology.

Matsushita inked the co-operation agreement with Philips. From then on, Matsushita was able to access easily the latest technology in Philips. The transfer agreement laid the groundwork for future development of Matsushita Corporation into a world-class company.

In business operation, it may not be bad to lose a little. The aim is to pursue a longer term interest and drive for future growth. This is the approach of a true general.

Art of Establishing Business Relationship and Negotiation

Section 2 The techniques of negotiation

> 兵者，诡道也。故能而示之不能，用而示之不用，近而示之远，远而示之近，利而诱之，乱而取之，实而备之，强而避之，怒而挠之，卑而骄之，佚而劳之，亲而离之，攻其无备，出其不意。此兵家之胜，不可先传也。
>
> Warfare is the way of deception.
> Therefore, if able, appear unable,
> if active, appear not active,
> if near, appear far,
> if far, appear near.
> If they have advantage, entice them;
> if they are confused, take them,
> if they are substantial, prepare for them,
> if they are strong, avoid them,
> if they are angry, disturb them,
> if they are humble, make them haughty,
> if they are relaxed, toil them,
> if they are united, separate them.
> Attack where they are not prepared, go out to where they do not expect.
> This specialized warfare leads to victory, and may not be transmitted beforehand.
>
> — *Chapter: Initial Assessment* 《始计篇》

Waging war is a test of tricks and deception. He who can fight will feign inability to fight. He who is to strike will feign not to strike. Those in the distant appear near while those near appear in a distant. If the enemy is eager to win, entice them. When the enemy is in disarray, attack them. If the enemy is strong, guard against them. When the enemy is powerful, avoid them. When the enemy is vigilant, agitate them. When the enemy is resting, perturb them. When the enemy is united, estrange them. In general, attack where least expected. This is the intricacy of controlling a war and cannot be decided in a dull and monotonous manner.

Since negotiation is part of planning for battle, we have to be vigilant in its strategy. The circumstance and strategy for negotiation change with different opponents and their psychology. In negotiation, the intelligence, charisma and approach of the negotiator will affect the opponent's way of thinking. The possession of information, domain knowledge and persuasiveness are important tools in negotiation. In general, business negotiation is to achieve a common ground and co-operate. There should not be confrontation in negotiation but to achieve a "win-win" situation.

The negotiator needs to influence and win over the opponent. He must first believe in the outcome and influence the negotiation towards achieving the outcome with the opponent. Sincerity is always the best strategy for negotiation. Sincerity cannot be replaced by intelligence or capability and neither can it be enforced through legal means.

Make use of different negotiation techniques.

Case Study 91: The Technique To Break A Deadlock Situation

Japan Matsushita Electric was negotiating with a European company. The negotiation reached a deadlock situation where both parties refused to make concessions. The negotiators were all fired up and the fiery negotiation was on the verge of collapse. A decision was made to adjourn for lunch and continue later.

I was at the science museum earlier and I saw a huge mould. I was nearly moved to tears by it. The quest of discovery for mankind is indeed admirable. There are now so many breakthroughs in science and technology.

I understand that Apollo 11 will soon go on another lunar voyage. The progress in knowledge and achievements made in science must be accredited to the hard work of mankind.

At the negotiation in the afternoon, Matsushita made his remarks.

However, human ties seem to have lagged behind compared to the progress made in science and technology. There is much mistrust and hatred among us. Many incidents of war and chaos arise out of the mistrust and hatred.

The endless line of people walking along the pedestrian walkway gives the impression that all is fine and peaceful. However, there is the conflict of our evil selves deep down in our hearts. Why can't the human relationship be more civil and cordial? I believe that there should be a fundamental trust, lesser mistake pointing and exploiting of weaknesses among us. We need a higher level of open-mindedness to build a better tomorrow!

The dizzying pace of technology advancement but languishing pace of civility will bring disaster to men. There is possibility of self-extermination of mankind with the atomic technology developed. The Japanese has painful experience of its power before…

At the beginning, the European negotiators were unmoved by Matsushita's words. Slowly, his words began to affect the audience and they resonated emotionally. There was a dramatic turn in negotiating atmosphere at the table. Both parties changed their attitudes from confrontation to partnership. The deadlock at negotiation was removed and the negotiation ended with a positive outcome.

There will always be deadlock situations in any negotiation. Under these situations, we need to look for common ground and strengthen the emotional link, thus creating a friendly atmosphere. Having a common ground brings conciliation to opposing views and unity in attitudes and interests. A common sentiment can break the deadlock, bringing new possibilities for a successful negotiation.

Chapter 10
Building a Corporate Culture

Section 1   Establish common ideals and team spirit

Section 2   Be a responsible corporate citizen

Building a Corporate Culture

Section 1　Establish common ideals and team spirit

> 上下同欲者胜
> One who knows how to unite upper and lower ranks in purpose will be victorious.
> 　　　　　　　　　— *Chapter: Attack by Stratagem* 《谋攻篇》
>
> 夫金鼓旌旗者，所以一人之耳目也。人既专一，则勇者不得独进，怯者不得独退，此用众之法也。
> Drums, gongs, flags, and pennants are used to unite men's eyes and ears.
> When the men are united, the brave cannot advance alone, the cowardly cannot retreat alone.
> These are the principles for employing a large number of troops.
> 　　　　　　　　　— *Chapter: Manoeuvring* 《军争篇》
>
> 善用兵者，避其锐气，击其惰归，此治气者也。
> Those skilled in the use of force avoid high energy, and strike when energy is exhausted.
> 　　　　　　　　　— *Chapter: Manoeuvring* 《军争篇》

Commanders and soldiers who share a common goal triumph.

　　Drums, pennants and flags are employed to unite the army. Once the soldiers are united, the courageous ones will not advance alone and the cowardly ones will not retreat alone. This is the way to command a large troop.

　　Those who are skilled in the art of warfare will steer clear from the initial confidence of the enemy before the battle and wait till their morale is low to commence an attack. This is mastery of the soldiers' morale.

　　Use a disciplined troop to provoke the chaotic enemy and a composed troop to hassle the frenzied enemy. This is mastery of the soldiers' psychology.

　　When the commanders and troops share a common value and objective, they will be victorious against the enemy. Having a united spirit will make the soldiers strong and overcome all obstacles. On the other hand, if the commanders and troops are disunited, the commander will lose control of the dispirited soldiers. Such an army is destined to fail.

　　There are many ways to build a corporate culture to achieve a "common goal". A "common goal" as a core value in a corporate culture can fit into any competitive environment. An excellent corporate culture creates common focus in objectives among employees. A common objective is formed by universal value and a desire to excel.

Case Study 92: A Universal Corporate Value

Shanghai Bao Shan Steel Company, formed in 1985, is the largest steel producing company in China. Although the history of the company is short, it has always been determined to establish a corporate culture. The vision of the company is to be a world-class steel making enterprise. The company's production techniques, technology and facilities have to be maintained at world-class standards. The company uses these objectives to foster a common value among its employees.

For example: the company's 80-ton automated transport truck had more than 100 positions and 50 other spots to lubricate. The lubricating work was targeted to be completed in less than 15 minutes. The inspection and repair work for the trucks involved more than 340 positions and 1,149 points. Forty-four of these positions and points had very small dimensions. The requirement was to complete the inspection within 70 minutes.

To achieve world-class standard, the workers were trained to carry out standardized work procedures.

Every inspection step must be done with military precision.

The highly disciplined workers always complete the tasks to the requirements even when the supervisor is not present.

The company further combined the individual work procedure into a department operating procedure where the work steps, requirements and work processes were unified. These standardization efforts created a company-wide "Best-in-Class" campaign. The departments made posters and charts to champion the goal of creating a best-in-class steel-making company. When the company began full scale production, there were already more than 369 standardized work flows.

The company assembled 1,200 technologists and engineers on a programme that promoted excellence in technology towards a world-class standard. The operators also formed work groups, facilitated by engineers, on quality improvement activities for the products. Excellence in quality thus became a supreme objective for the company.

The company had once outsourced a batch of steel pipes to a small contractor to form the necessary piping bends. Cracks were later found on some of these pipe bends (which could possibly be due to pipe quality or the bending process). Upon receiving complaints from customers, the management promptly made a decision. Ship the pipes back and find out the root cause. Send a new batch of pipes to the customers and all expenses will be absorbed by the company. This incident shall serve as a useful lesson to the employees on the importance of quality and good reputation for the company.

A healthy corporate culture inculcates unity among employees. When everyone sets his goal on a common target, it infuses positive effect for the company's growth and operation.

Case Study 93: The Uniquely "HP Way"

The corporate culture at Hewlett Packard is also known as the "HP Way". The "HP Way" is the key for the technology company to overcome poor economy and achieve sustained growth.

The co-founder of HP, William Hewlett said this about the "HP Way":

The tradition of HP is to position management in the shoes of employees. We respect our employees and recognize each one's contribution. We may sound like singing an old tune but we religiously hold on to this belief. The dignity and value of each employee is an integral part of the "HP Way".

The company abolished the punch card system many years ago. Now, we move a step further to implement the flexible working hours arrangement. We trust that our employees are capable of managing official working hours and personal time well.

Everyone calls each other by his/her name. The core value, encompassing the "HP Way", is to respect all employees.

The company announced: HP does not have a regimental work structure but allows our employees the freedom to decide the best way to perform in their work.

With the organization of HP, it does not matter that the employee is an engineer or a technician. He is allowed to bring storage devices home from the company's laboratory, whether the device is for personal use or company's work. The company believes that the more an employee uses an item or equipment, the better is his competency at work. It will also help to enhance the company's innovation capacity.

Once, William Hewlett was at the office on a weekend. He found that the store room of the laboratory was locked up. He was infuriated.

Get the locksmith. immediately!!

When the employees returned to work the following Monday, they saw a note left behind by William Hewlett. The faith and trust he has in his employees greatly encouraged initiatives at work in HP.

Never lock this place ever again!!

Employees at every HP office are earnestly discussing how to improve the quality of their products. They are extremely proud of the great achievements at HP. A strong sense of commitment and spirit can be seen in everyone.

The trust, respect and care for employees in HP has created the uniquely "HP Way".

Case Study 94: The Core Values At Matsushita

In 1936, Matsushita Konosuke put together the seven core principles at Matsushita Company.

1. Contribution to Society
2. Fairness and Honesty
3. Cooperation and Team Spirit
4. Untiring Effort for Improvement
5. Courtesy and Humility
6. Adaptability
7. Gratitude

The success of Matsushita is built largely on the seven core principles. Matsushita Konosuke avowed the corporate principles with the following core values in mind: "Understand the responsibility of an entrepreneur. Encourage improvement at work. Help to improve the welfare of society and development of global culture".

The motto at Matsushita is: "Progress and development can be realized only through the combined efforts and cooperation of each employee of our company. United in spirit, we pledge to perform our corporate duties with dedication, diligence and integrity".

Matsushita emphasized the need to instill the company's core values into its employees. At eight o'clock in the morning, all 87,000 employees in Japan would recite the core values and sing aloud the company's song. This song was composed by Matsushita Konosuke. Matsushita Company is the first Japanese company that has its own core values and company song.

Matsushita Konosuke wanted his department managers to be clear in giving instructions. He also strongly believed that new recruits are the future of the company. Matsushita Konosuke was bold in his employment practice. For an employee with high integrity, Matsushita would give him heavier responsibilities so that he could develop his potential. The trust and responsibility would be independent of the education level and work experience.

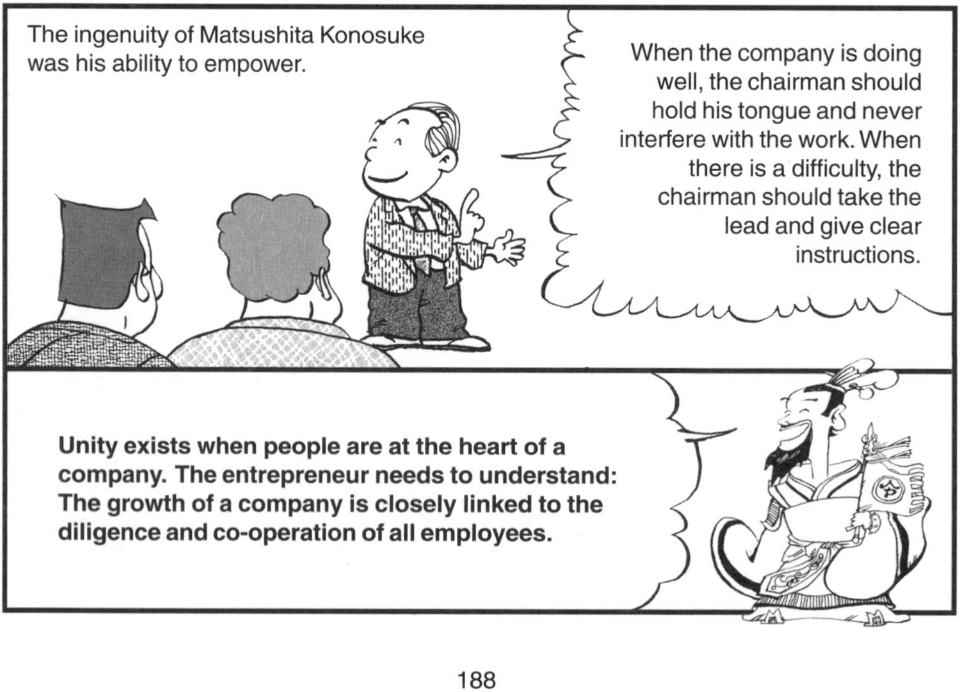

The ingenuity of Matsushita Konosuke was his ability to empower.

When the company is doing well, the chairman should hold his tongue and never interfere with the work. When there is a difficulty, the chairman should take the lead and give clear instructions.

Unity exists when people are at the heart of a company. The entrepreneur needs to understand: The growth of a company is closely linked to the diligence and co-operation of all employees.

Case Study 95: Putting The Company In Order

ITT Corp was once an exceptional American company in the international phone business. In 1959, the general manager, Harold Geneen, began a corporate re-engineering to revamp the company.

Most of the executives at its subsidiaries were supportive of his effort but there were a few managers who wanted to have their own way.

Let's do something about these black sheep!

The French subsidiary manager, Danfield was a stubborn man and refused to submit monthly reports despite repeated reminders.

I am the nephew of the company director, Biederman. What can you possibly do to me?

Danfield is to be relinquished of all his duties and a new branch manager is appointed with immediate effect.

Geneen made an announcement.

Danfield refused to accept the announcement. The new manager was asked by Geneen to look for a new office and made an official company announcement in the newspapers.

Employees who report to work at the new office will continue to be employed. Those who refuse to show up will be terminated!

With the ultimatum printed blatantly in thenewspapers, Danfield had no choice but to accept the reality. Geneen was steadfast and clear in his corporate re-engineering stance. He was successful in his restructuring effort.

Case Study 96: Upkeeping Law And Order

Ito Trading had its beginnings in the textile industry and was a strong player. However, the food business was lagging in its stable of businesses. To help establish the business, Kishishin Ichio was headhunted from its competitor, Higashi Shoku, to head the food department.

Higashi Shoku specialised in food trading business. Kishishin was a veteran with the company. After making his move to Ito Trading, he helped the food department achieve outstanding results.

The chairman of Ito Trading, Ito Masatoshi, was a traditional man and emphasised on discipline within an organization. He opposed the use of entertainment as leverage for business. Kishishin believed otherwise. He spent excessively on entertainment and was lax on his subordinates' entertainment expenditure.

Masatoshi advised Kishishin to change his business style and follow the company's established business process. Kishinshin, however, continued in his old ways. The food business grew too.

Why change when all is well?

The differences in beliefs deepened as the days went by. The internal strife caused a ruffle and affected other departments. Masatoshi had no choice but to exercise what he thought was right.

Terminate Kishishin!

To remove Kishishin on impulse is incorrect and inhumane!

Masatoshi is unscrupulous!

Masatoshi's decision shocked the industry and incurred much criticism.

Even though the food department was highly profitable under Kishishin's leadership, his practices were against the company's established processes. To turn a blind eye would undermine the company's system and foundation. This would affect the survival of the company. Order needs to take precedence over humanity.

Building a Corporate Culture

Section 2 Be a responsible corporate citizen

> 计利以听，乃为之势，以佐其外。势者，因利而制权也。
> Calculate advantages by means of what was heard, then create force in order to assist outside missions.
> Force is the control of the balance of power, in accordance with advantages.
> — *Chapter: Initial Assessment* 《始计篇》
>
> 故善战者，求之于势，不责于人故能择人而任势。
> Those skilled in warfare seek victory through force and do not require too much from individuals.
> Therefore, they are able to select the right men and exploit force.
> — *Chapter: Use of Military Momentum* 《兵势篇》

After the correct strategy has been decided, one needs to create an advantageous position in the progress of the battle. A person skilled in commanding a battle would create an advantageous position that is like falling rocks from a mountain which grows in strength and intensity. This is known as "force".

For the survival and development of a company, the changing society and public opinions are comparable to the vast ocean and navigation compass. A company that is operating with a good social image and is well received by the public will be like a ship sailing in calm waters. It is in an advantageous position. On the contrary, a bad social image would bring resentment and rejection from the public. This is similar to paddling against the tide in a treacherous sea. Hence, while the company is developing its strength, it also needs to "create awareness" of the external and internal influences for the company.

Currently, there is more awareness of corporate responsibility towards the society. The awareness comes in the wake of a greater recognition that while a company needs to be profitable, there are also responsibilities towards the environment, society and other stakeholders that cannot be overlooked. A growing company cannot pursue a sole purpose of making profit. It needs to be aware of its corporate moral principles, improvement in workers' working conditions and benefits to the society.

A company needs to establish its reputation for a sustained development, with consideration for the environment. This has become an irreversible trend in society.

The company has to listen to the callings of the society and expectations of the public while creating its identity.

Case Study 97: Social Awareness Management System 8000 (SA8000)

In the 1990s, social awareness campaign took prominence among many international companies. The campaign was initiated by an American non-government organization, Social Awareness International (SAI). This campaign advocated that companies be responsible for the impact their business activities had on the society. The impact could range from environmental issues to social impact on stakeholders. After 2000, almost all American and European companies have enforced an audit on the level of social awareness in their suppliers and contractors. Only companies that passed the audit are able to establish a supply partnership. Many corporations, like Nike, Adidas, Walmart and McDonalds, joined the social awareness movement. They established an internal code of conduct and made it compulsory for their supply chain partners to have the same code of conduct.

SA8000's primary concerns cover the following areas: 1. the problem of child labour; 2. the problem of forced labour; 3. health and safety at work; 4. freedom to form unions and rights for collective bargaining; 5. fight against discrimination; 6. punishments and penalties; 7. working hours; 8. salary and compensation; 9. administrative system

The area of audit included: production line, workers' accommodation, warehouse, workers' canteen, health facilities, site inspection, traffic, work and rest hours, changes in workers' shifts. Documentations included: personal particulars of employees, records of payments and salaries, labour contracts; production records, industrial accident statistics. As of May 2004, 400 organizations from 40 countries and different industries were certified as complying to the standards. A total of 260,000 employees were involved.

There was an incident of cancellation of orders in a shoes factory in Guangzhou. This cancellation was due to a food poisoning case at the factory. The factory was on the verge of collapse with the overwhelming cancellation of orders. Ever since it was reported in July 2003, more than 30 concerned customers called daily to enquire and they demanded an improvement in work conditions for the factory workers.

In contrast to the alarming cancellation of orders at the shoes factory, assistant general manager of Shen Zhen Xing Wei Metal and Plastic Private Limited, Song Zhi Minq was calm and confident.

We officially achieved SA8000 certification on 1 February 2004. Within half a year, we see our orders increased two-fold from the quantity in 2003.

H&M is the largest fashion retail chain in Sweden. It has 994 retail shops in 19 countries around the world. More than 3,000 garment factories, located in different regions worldwide, are suppliers of fashion wear to the company. Direct suppliers to the company are close to 900.

For all its suppliers, H&M listed a concrete set of code of conduct in 1997. In the stated code of conduct, every supplier has to pay the minimum salary and provide the necessary workplace safety protection for its workers. The company translated the code of conduct into 25 languages and distributed the multi-language booklets to all its suppliers. It went a step further to employ 30 auditors to make yearly audits on the suppliers. In 2003, more than 2,000 audits were conducted. Among these audits, one-third of the inspections were surprise audits without prior notification to the suppliers.

The social awareness system has enhanced the sense of responsibility companies should have towards the environment and society at large. It creates a harmonious relationship for legitimate and law-abiding companies with the society. It is a campaign that should be strongly promoted.

Case Study 98: Honda Bravely Confronted Market Problems

In the 1960s, the world automobile market was dominated by a few big players. Japan's Honda was then a new entrant.

There are many good players in the industry. Honda can never become a true competitor by imitating others' products. We need to have innovative technology and high-quality products to win over the customers.

The automobile engine was still in the early stage of development. Many cars began to jam the streets and corners of the cities. City dwellers started protesting against the noise and air pollution.

Honda decided to develop a car that would create less pollution. This became the company's top priority. Honda aggressively invested manpower and resources into the project. In 1972, Honda launched a low-pollution engine that passed the requirements in the newly enacted Muskie Anti-pollution Act in United States of America.

In 1973, the new Honda vehicle with low-pollution engine was introduced to consumers and that immediately won praises. This was also a defining moment for Honda to be among the leaders of automobile technology and production. Honda cars were in high demand all over the world. Other car makers came to Honda to seek co-operation or technology transfer.

Honda noticed the market needs and decisively invested to develop technology know-how for the company. This move enabled the company to transform into a technology leader that others were keen to learn from.

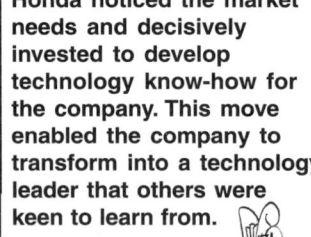

Case Study 99: The Most Successful Corporate Crisis Communication

On 30 September 1982, seven individuals died in metropolitan Chicago after criminals tampered and laced cyanide into the Extra Strength Tylenol capsules which can be bought over the counter at pharmaceutical stores. The popular painkiller was produced by Johnson & Johnson. This put Johnson & Johnson's 40 years of pharmaceutical legacy in jeopardy. The company promptly activated its crisis public relations communication procedures.

1. Inform the Food and Drug Administration. Recall the capsules in 31 states for immediate destruction.
2. Alert the consumers by sending out 450,000 telecommunication messages to medicines retailers and pharmacies.
3. Set up a hotline to answer queries. Inform the media.

4. Request the World Health Organization to notify global medicines and pharmaceutical distributors of the incident.
5. Stop all production of Tylenol capsules from 30 September to mid October.

At normal times, Johnson & Johnson would receive 700 to 800 enquiries from the media yearly. During this crisis in October 1982, the number of enquiries shot up to more than 2,000. The company faithfully recorded all news reports. Within a few months, the company had records of more than 2,500 reports and also other information of enquirers. Johnson & Johnson maintained a close contact with these enquirers. This was a crucial move in its cause-finding effort.

In November 1982, one month after the incident, the company organized a news conference that was broadcast "live" to more than 30 cities. At the conference, Tylenol capsules were reintroduced bearing a new triple-seal tamper-proof packaging. James E. Burke, chairman of the board at the time of the tamperings was more than willing in his answers to the media. After the media conference, Johnson & Johnson handed out 8 million Tylenol discount vouchers.

The handout invited more than 430,000 customers who called the hotline Within a year, Tylenol capsules made a comeback and earned 80 percent market share.

The communication procedure at the crisis was carried out according to the following principles: "Responsibility towards consumers", "Protection in the interest of consumers", "Factual information to the public". Johnson & Johnson, in executing the procedures, recalled and destroyed the tainted capsules; informed the public to regain their trust; and made factual disclosure to the media and won their support.

Public relations is a fundamental issue to a company. It is the window of the company for outsiders. The image and reputation to the general public are the bed-rock and lifeline of a company. A company needs to plan for contingencies and establish a complete public relations strategy.

Case Study 100: Bring Benefits To Society And Establish A Positive Image

The environment problem is an important issue facing the world today. For Nokia's sustained growth, it followed a strict environmental policy that is applicable to its operations worldwide. The environment policy at Nokia is also built into the product life cycle. Throughout the product's stages in life; starting from product design, material selection, production operation, after-sales services and finally returned goods, environmental impact by each operation is carefully considered.

Nokia phone design is highly friendly to the environment. At the early stage of product design, environment friendly attributes are built into the product. This approach produces a product that requires minimum materials to make and consumed the lowest possible power. The environment protection awareness and knowledge have become an integral part of employees' training. This fosters an awareness of the relationship between employees' work and environment protection.

The effort in protecting the environment at Nokia has won worldwide acceptance and respect. In 2003, Nokia was ranked first for sustained growth and performance among European companies' component stocks in Dow Jones Index. It was also the best performer among all telecommunication companies.

Nokia, in striving to achieve business excellence, has not forgotten its responsibility towards the society. In every country Nokia operates in, it relentlessly works towards the goal of becoming a model corporate citizen and it participates actively in local community services.

Nokia provided special funding to help street urchins who have been living off the streets of Mexico.

In Britain, Nokia participated in a campaign that aimed at helping the intellectually disabled. In Brazil, Nokia set up an education fund that promoted learning of telecommunication and information technology for local students.

In 1998, Nokia sponsored two events, namely "The '98 China International Arts Exhibition" in China and "Exhibition on 5,000 years in Chinese Civilization" in New York, USA. In 2001, Nokia became the only telecommunication company that sponsored the 21st World University Games. Between 2000 and 2002, Nokia worked with the Chinese government in a country-wide programme in tree and green planting. The effort paid off with an extra 300,000 square metres of green space in China by 2004.

> A progressive company needs self-restraint and contribute to the society, while pursuing profit interest. Establish an excellent corporate image and reputation in favour of a long term development and a "win-win" outcome.

Sunzi's Art of War

Chapter 1   **Initial Assessments** 《始计篇》
Before winning a battle, start planning first
决胜於庙堂之上

Chapter 2   **Waging War** 《作战篇》
A war should be won quickly without being prolonged
兵以速胜，不宜持久

Chapter 3   **Attack by Stratagem** 《谋攻篇》
To subdue the enemy without fighting is perfect victory
不战而使敌人屈服的胜利最完美

Chapter 4   **Disposition of Military Forces** 《军形篇》
Never go to war unprepared
全面准备，胜兵先胜

Chapter 5   **Formation** 《兵势篇》
Creating favourable conditions and seizing the opportunity to win
军旅攻击，正合奇胜

Chapter 6   **Weaknesses and Strengths** 《虚实篇》
Be adept at moving the enemy to where you wish instead of being moved by the enemy
致人而不致於人

Chapter 7   **Manoeuvring** 《军争篇》
Convert unfavourable factors into favourable ones and seize the opportunity to fight
以迂为直，以患为利

Chapter 8 **Nine Variations of Tactics** 《九变篇》
Make flexible adjustment of tactics according to changing circumstances of the battlefield
为将之道

Chapter 9 **Mobilisation** 《行军篇》
Marching, camping and observation of the battlefields
处军相敌，发挥战力

Chapter 10 **The Terrain** 《地形篇》
The military geography should not be neglected
军事地理，不容忽视

Chapter 11 **Nine Types of Strategic Ground** 《九地篇》
To stage a surprise attack against the enemy and penetrate deeply into the enemy territory
胜敌之地，主客之道

Chapter 12 **Attack with Fire** 《火攻篇》
Act from inside in coordination with forces attacking from outside assisted by fire
以火助攻，里应外合

Chapter 13 **Intelligence** 《用间篇》
Strategic reconnaissance is essential in war
知敌之情，至关重要

Sunzi's Art of War, the revised edition published by Asiapac Books, includes the original Chinese text. It covers widely the subject of strategizing. Containing extensive knowledge, dealt with in great depth, it is a crystallization of human wisdom, and has the potential to change the direction the world is heading. Its influence is felt not only in state administration, but also in business management, public relations and diplomacy, and even sports. Thus we can see how flexibly Sun Wu's strategizing principles can be applied, making it a resource for anyone desiring to meet any challenge.

ISBN: 981-3068-99-X

Business Strategies

Golden Rules for Business Success
Tao Zhugong propounds on 12 Golden Standards and 12 Golden Safeguards for business success in a competitive world.

Chinese Business Strategies
The secret of Chinese business success lies in 10 time-tested principles of entrepreneurship. Includes 30 real life case studies.

Sun Bin's Art of War: World's Greatest Military Treatise
The household Chinese name Sunzi refers to the great military strategist Sun Wu, as well as his descendant Sun Bin, who was framed and crippled but went on to win countless wars and to write the brilliant *Art of War*. Be inspired by his tenacity and wisdom.

100 Strategies of War: Brilliant Tactics in Action
This book captures the essence of extensive military knowledge and practice, and explores the use of psychology in warfare, the importance of diplomatic ties with the enemy's neighbours, and the use of reconnaissance and espionage.

Thirty-six Stratagems: Secret Art of War
A Chinese military classic that emphasises deceptive schemes to achieve military objectives, this book has caught the attention of military authorities and general readers alike.

Sixteen Strategies: The Art of Management
With advice on how a king should govern the country, establish harmonious relations with his subjects and use reward and punishment to win his people's trust, this is a boon for those involved in business management.

Strategies from the Three Kingdoms
The war stratagems and military teachings which emerged from the Three Kingdoms Period have influenced the way later generations view leadership and power.

36 Business Stratagems: Secret Art of War for Today's Entrepreneurs
Some 100 case studies show you how business people win over customers and stay agile in a fast-changing business environment.

Seven Military Classics

by Wang Xuanming

Sunzi's Art of War: World's Most Famous Military Classic
This famous military classic covers the full spectrum of strategising. Containing extensive knowledge, dealt with in great depth, it is a crystallisation of human wisdom.

Sima's Rules of War: The Practice of Dynamic Leadership
Famed War Minister Tian Rangju shares his experience in planning for campaigns, handling warfare, strategising for victory and much more!

Three Strategies of Huang Shi Gong: The Art of Government
Reputedly one of man's oldest monograph on military strategy, it unmasks the secrets behind brilliant military manoeuvres, clever deployment and control of subordinates, as well as effective government.

Six Strategies for War: The Practice of Effective Leadership
A powerful book for administrators and leaders, it covers critical areas in management and warfare. These include how to recruit talents, manage the state, beat the enemy, lead wisely and manoeuvre brilliantly.

The Art of Winning: Wisdom of Tang Tai Zong and Duke Li of Wei
In question-and-answer format, this war-wise emperor and his intrepid commander take us through the logic of winning battles, analysing examples drawn from their own experience and from history's famous battles.

The Art of Tactics: Winning Strategies of Wu Zi
Wu Zi, who was praised by famed Legalist Li Li for surpassing Sima Rangju and Sun Zi, was superb at translating strategies into action. He delves into topics like resolving tactical situations, evaluating the enemy, responding to change, and stimulating one's followers.

The Art of Command: Wei Liao Zi's Strategies of War
Wei Liao was an astute political observer and brilliant strategist with a superb grasp of civil and military measures critical to a state's survival. His work has been hailed as a distinguished work of military science with principles on par with Sun Zi's.

Leadership

The Art of Goal Setting
Illustrates the strategies used by the ancients to achieve the feats that challenge even modern imagination. Ideal for personal and group use.

Gems of Chinese Wisdom
Find out how to use wisdom in understanding, observation, decision-making and forming principles for the conduct of business and relationships. Learn from the likes of Confucius, Meng Changjun and many others.

Strategies from the Three Kingdoms
Be resourceful and versatile, have resilience and vision, anticipate the opponent's move, know your competitor... These age-old strategies are the epitome of wisdom.

Chinese Wisdom on Life & Management
Demonstrates how the five dimensions of Universal Oneness — the Principles of Unity, Opposites, Cycle, Balance and Change — have empowered business leaders.

Visit us at
www.asiapacbooks.com
for more information on Asiapac titles.

You will find:
- ▲ Asiapac - The Company
- ▲ Asiapac Logo
- ▲ Asiapac Publications
- ▲ Comics Extracts
- ▲ Book Reviews
- ▲ New Publications
- ▲ Ordering Our Publications

Culture · Strategy & Leadership · Philosophy · History · English Language Reader Magazines · Language

To order books or write to us:
asiapacbooks@pacific.net.sg

全胜：孙子商法实例100则

编绘 ：王宣铭

翻译 ：符祝炎

亚太图书有限公司出版